NEW DIRECTIONS FOR COMMUNITY COLLEGES

Arthur M. Cohen
EDITOR-IN-CHIEF

Florence B. Brawer
ASSOCIATE EDITOR

Erika Yamasaki
PUBLICATION COORDINATOR

Gateways to Democracy: Six Urban Community College Systems

Raymond C. Bowen
LaGuardia Community College

Gilbert H. Muller
LaGuardia Community College

EDITORS

Number 107, Fall 1999

JOSSEY-BASS PUBLISHERS
San Francisco

NOV 1 5

Gateways to democracy

GATEWAYS TO DEMOCRACY: SIX URBAN COMMUNITY COLLEGE SYSTEMS
Raymond C. Bowen, Gilbert H. Muller (eds.)
New Directions for Community Colleges, no. 107
Volume XXVII, number 3
Arthur M. Cohen, Editor-in-Chief
Florence B. Brawer, Associate Editor

New Directions for Community Colleges is indexed in Current Index to Journals in Education (ERIC).

Microfilm copies of issues and articles are available in 16mm and 35mm, as well as microfiche in 105mm, through University Microfilms Inc., 300 North Zeeb Road, Ann Arbor, Michigan 48106-1346.

ISSN 0194-3081   ISBN 0-7879-4848-9

NEW DIRECTIONS FOR COMMUNITY COLLEGES is part of The Jossey-Bass Higher and Adult Education Series and is published quarterly by Jossey-Bass Inc., Publishers, 350 Sansome Street, San Francisco, California 94104-1342, in association with the ERIC Clearinghouse for Community Colleges. Periodicals postage paid at San Francisco, California, and at additional mailing offices. POSTMASTER: Send address changes to New Directions for Community Colleges, Jossey-Bass Inc., Publishers, 350 Sansome Street, San Francisco, California 94104-1342.

SUBSCRIPTIONS cost $60.00 for individuals and $107.00 for institutions, agencies, and libraries. Prices subject to change.

THE MATERIAL in this publication is based on work sponsored wholly or in part by the Office of Educational Research and Improvement, U.S. Department of Education, under contract number RI-93-00-2003. Its contents do not necessarily reflect the views of the Department or any other agency of the U.S. Government.

EDITORIAL CORRESPONDENCE should be sent to the Editor-in-Chief, Arthur M. Cohen, at the ERIC Clearinghouse for Community Colleges, University of California, 3051 Moore Hall, Box 951521, Los Angeles, California 90095-1521. All manuscripts receive anonymous reviews by external referees.

Cover photograph © Rene Sheret, After Image, Los Angeles, California, 1990.

www.josseybass.com

Printed in the United States of America on acid-free recycled paper containing 100 percent recovered waste paper, of which at least 20 percent is postconsumer waste.

CONTENTS

EDITORS' NOTES

Urban community colleges play multiple and challenging roles in the social, political, and economic fabric of the nation's metropolitan areas. From New York to Los Angeles, community colleges in urban settings strive to provide equal access and opportunity to all individuals and, increasingly, to meet the educational and training needs of diverse ethnic and racial groups. This volume features case studies of six prototypical urban community college systems and an overview of the key challenges they face. A chapter detailing sources and information is included as a resource for those seeking additional material. The chapters provide a useful guide for practitioners, public policy advocates, and scholars interested in the unique missions of the nation's urban institutions.

Preliminary research reveals a paucity of scholarship on urban community colleges. In fact, the definition of a two-year urban institution of higher education is still evolving. The stipulative definition that the authors develop throughout this volume is that the urban community college is committed to addressing the needs and expectations of nontraditional, increasingly nonwhite and immigrant, and relatively disenfranchised metropolitan constituencies. Such a definition embraces perhaps 150 colleges in the United States, although twice this number probably classify themselves as urban in design, function, and spirit. For example, there is growing evidence (as shown by the chapters on Seattle and Baltimore) that urbanization is not necessarily confined to geographic locations that traditionally have been considered metropolitan or urban. As formerly suburban areas are being transformed, institutions in these locales also need to serve ethnically diverse, underrepresented populations. In essence, an urban community college serves racially and ethnically diverse populations—"majority minorities"—who reflect a central reality of urban demographics today but often live on the margins of American society. These students, as Mike Rose observes in his 1989 award-winning book, lead "lives on the boundary," the title of his semiautobiographical odyssey through urban America. As such, a significant component of our stipulative definition requires consideration of social, political, and economic matters centering on issues of class, race, and ethnicity.

The definition of urban community colleges as institutions situated in major cities or contiguous areas, having urban characteristics, and serving historically poor and underrepresented populations guides this volume. The case studies that present community college systems from the City University of New York (CUNY) and Miami-Dade to those in Los Angeles and Seattle focus on a common set of concerns:

Which campuses within the system are urban and which quasi-urban or sub-urban?
What challenges do poverty, race, immigration, and other demographic trends pose for urban community colleges?
How can urban systems serve as academic links between public secondary schools and four-year institutions?
How do urban community colleges contribute to community service and economic development?
What are the impacts of city, state, and federal forces on the vitality of urban community colleges and the constituencies they serve?

These issues highlight the tensions between the promise of the urban community college mission and the real problems impinging on that mission.

The contributors to this volume assert from various perspectives that urban community colleges have the potential to serve as political agents of change and mobility for large metropolitan constituencies, as well as academic agents striving to meet the educational needs of individuals. The task is daunting; recent systemic crises at CUNY and the Los Angeles Community College District suggest that the future of urban community colleges will tell us much about the United States in the twenty-first century. As we imply in this volume, the reconciliation of disparate educational and social functions will be the key challenge for urban community college leaders for the future.

The chapters in this volume look at six of the most interesting urban community colleges in the United States. These case studies are preceded in Chapter One by Joshua L. Smith and Fayyaz A. Vellani's assessment of the current national urban situation; they reiterate the need to preserve an urban mission constantly threatened by political, economic, and social forces. In Chapter Two, Eduardo J. Padrón and Theodore Levitt examine the Miami-Dade system and the adjustments being made to address emerging demographic trends in southern Florida. In Chapter Three, Joanne Reitano analyzes the six community colleges within CUNY and the severe pressures they currently confront. In Chapter Four, Julie Yearsley Hungar traces the evolution of the Seattle community college system and its investment in the urban mission. In Chapter Five, Jack Fujimoto offers an overview of the Los Angeles Community College District and its efforts to provide access while strengthening accountability. In Chapter Six, Paul A. Elsner assesses Arizona's Maricopa Community College District's ongoing conversation over its mission and purpose. In Chapter Seven, Irving Pressley McPhail and Ronald C. Heacock examine the multicampus Community College of Baltimore County, a system in transition from suburban to increasingly urban contours. Chapter Eight provides an annotated list of the recent literature on urban community colleges by Dana Scott Peterman and Carol A. Kozeracki.

Within the urban sector of higher education, community colleges serve as gateways to democracy for the nation's increasingly diverse citizenry. The purpose of this volume is to illuminate and reaffirm the pathways to access and accomplishment that urban community colleges continue to forge.

Raymond C. Bowen ˙
Gilbert H. Muller
Editors

RAYMOND C. BOWEN is president of LaGuardia Community College, New York.

GILBERT H. MULLER is special assistant to the president at LaGuardia Community College, New York.

1

Urban community colleges have unique missions geared to providing access and fostering community for the diverse student populations—majority minorities—living today in American cities.

Urban America and the Community College Imperative: The Importance of Open Access and Opportunity

Joshua L. Smith, Fayyaz A. Vellani

A visit to almost any community college in the metropolitan United States would reveal a gathering of students from around the world. Some days the hubbub and excitement on these campuses approximate the atmosphere of an airport's international arrivals terminal. These institutions serve as gateways to higher education for students from myriad ethnic and racial backgrounds, many representing what scholars term the "fourth wave" of immigration to the United States. Together with nontraditional native students, these immigrants are using the resources of urban community colleges to prepare for employment in the new century.

From Melting Pot to Mosaic

Students have discovered that America's urban community colleges offer a chance to learn about other cultures and obtain the knowledge and skills needed to move ahead in careers. Urban community colleges are truly the academic arenas where citizens who will populate the cities of the twenty-first century are learning what it takes to live and work in diverse metropolitan settings.

At these colleges, students garner more than skills and knowledge that will help them enter the workplace or transfer to four-year colleges. They comprehensively begin to extract valuable civic knowledge and cultural cues that allow them to navigate successfully in a democratic nation in the era of late capitalism, as defined by Fredric Jameson (1991). Interacting meaningfully with people who are different requires the recognition of incredible demographic diversity, especially in urban areas.

The demographics of many American cities show a high percentage of immigrants and people of color. Typically more than half of the students at two-year campuses in New York, Chicago, Los Angeles, and elsewhere consist of "majority minorities." At the Community College of Denver (CCD), for example, 1997–98 enrollment data show a student body that is 9 percent Asian, 13 percent African American, 32 percent Hispanic, 2 percent Native American, 45 percent white, and 3 percent international. CCD's mission statement reads: "Community College of Denver is a comprehensive, student-centered urban college, providing access to a diverse population." Urban community colleges like CCD, as Richardson (1984) asserts, can be distinguished from the vast majority of the nation's twelve hundred two-year institutions in terms of their settings, clientele, and importance to the communities they serve.

For the most part, students who attend urban community colleges have to work to make ends meet. Many are married and support families. Their responsibilities keep them very focused. The students' work ethic and the learning environments these community colleges provide all work to strengthen the economic and civic fabric of cities. In the process, students are mainstreamed into the local economy. Often they sustain or revitalize inner-city areas, as in the case of LaGuardia Community College in New York, which has spearheaded the transformation of a formerly depressed section of western Queens. Similar inner-city revivals, spurred by the central location of urban community colleges, can be found in Pittsburgh, Dallas, Jacksonville, and elsewhere (Weidenthal, 1989).

American Cities and the American Dream

Urban community colleges are predicated on open admissions and access, both under assault in systems from New York to Chicago to Los Angeles. As Inez Martinez (interview, Mar. 29, 1999) asserts:

> Open admissions has been and remains the path to pursuit of the American dream for students who otherwise know little hope. It has meant that higher education and all its enablements no longer belong only to the elite: the elite of wealth or the elite of what this culture has measured as intelligence. It has meant that the vast majority of people, including the poor, the immigrant, the working classes, people of color and females, all get an opportunity to pursue their life, liberty and happiness.

Urban two-year colleges can no longer be considered marginal institutions; they are core institutions that serve a great need in this nation's cities.

Urban community colleges enroll a higher proportion of minorities than their suburban and rural two-year counterparts or most universities. As such, they are truly, as David Pierce (1999) asserts, the "democracy colleges" at which a broad range of people choose to obtain their education. At a time when the condition of many cities is often dire, urban community colleges equip people with skills to take up jobs that will improve lives, communities, and economies.

Since the early 1900s in the United States, the movement of people from east to west has been accompanied by the movement from farms to cities. Following World War II, which greatly stimulated industrial growth in the North and the West, migration escalated from rural areas of the South and Midwest toward the cities, where people found jobs in the factories that were fueling an expanding economy. Meanwhile, the development of the suburban ring around cities, fostered by commuter railroads and trolley lines in the 1920s, accelerated again as large numbers of people moved into suburban areas. Simultaneously, federally subsidized mortgages for veterans, the births of the baby boomers, and the federal Interstate Highway Act promoted an exodus from core cities to suburban and exurban areas in the 1950s, 1960s, and 1970s. The tide, though, left many behind, often because of poverty, race, and language. The population shifts continue as the states of the old midwestern farm and industrial belts continue to decline in population while cities in the Sunbelt grow rapidly. The tide has resulted in the megacity, whose political units may be fragmented but are bound together in "Bos-Wash," "Gary-Chicago-Milwaukee," "Los Angeles–Long Beach," and "Miami–Fort Lauderdale" (Hodgkinson, 1996). Within these cities and megacities, urban community colleges—whether located in the older Rust Belt, like Cuyahoga Community College in Cleveland, or in the Sun Belt, like the Maricopa system in Phoenix—struggle to provide further education for the members of their communities.

It is also notable, as William Gray (1999) indicates, that by the year 2000, one-third of the workforce will be composed of people of color, immigrants, and women. By 2050, 50 percent of the population will be immigrant and/or nonwhite. In fact, immigration has created such a polyglot urban society that the conventional classifications of race and ethnicity are now obsolete (Carter, 1998). New York City is a prime example of a municipality that maintains its population through immigration. As Cheng (1998) notes, New York's loss of population through migration has been and will continue to be offset by high numbers of immigrants from foreign countries.

Cohen and Brawer (1989) observed, "Community colleges in cities with high populations of minorities—Chicago, Cleveland, El Paso, Los Angeles, Miami, New York, Phoenix—enroll large numbers of minority students. At East Los Angeles College in the mid 1980s, 65 percent of the students were Hispanic; at Los Angeles Southwest College, 87 percent were black" (p. 43).

Urban community colleges, unlike any other institution in American higher education, have become the "common school" that Horace Mann envisioned in the 1830s and 1840s. By serving all of the people, including immigrants and other historically disenfranchised and underrepresented groups, urban community colleges provide the common educational ground on which people from various backgrounds come together to acquire skills for work and citizenship.

Urban Missions and Urban Challenges

Simple arithmetic is forcing urban community colleges to face problems that are unique in history and for which there appear to be no acceptable solutions. In the 1960s and 1970s, the challenge was to provide the space and open the doors to accommodate the large number of students seeking higher education. The current task is to assume a major role in serving the new populations. Unlike other institutions, these community colleges are not yet bound by tradition and thus can be more flexible while remaining true to their mission of providing instruction in the liberal arts and sciences, occupational education, remedial education, continuing education, and open access to anyone possessing a high school diploma or its equivalent. In California, for example, access to community colleges is guaranteed by law to anyone over the age of eighteen with the ability to benefit from instruction.

As the emphasis on one portion of the mission or the other has shifted since the 1960s, so too has the nature of the student body. More students with poor collegiate preparation are entering urban community colleges, a fact often seen as a negative. In meeting the needs of these students, the urban community college has blazed a trail in building partnerships with precollegiate education. Simultaneously, the colleges are working with students who are long out of high school, offering them a set of remedial courses that provide them with the skills necessary for successful college-level work.

Increasingly, urban community colleges are being challenged to justify what they do. Concerns have been raised about students' graduation rates, transfer rates, and time to complete a degree. In some states, policymakers are questioning the efficacy of remediation while at the same time requiring entrance examinations for admission to community colleges, thus completely transforming their missions.

Moreover, many critics of the urban community college point accusatory fingers at the colleges for emphasizing vocational education or for failing to produce large numbers of graduates who attain the baccalaureate degree. Using the baccalaureate as the criterion of success ignores the goal of many underrepresented populations and immigrants to gain a foothold in the economic system. Urban community colleges, which are gateways for nontraditional and immigrant populations, should be proud that they produce graduates who join the workforce. Moreover, as David E. Lavin (1981, 1996) has demonstrated in his studies of open admissions at the City University of New York, urban college students persist in significant numbers to obtain the associate and bachelor's degrees, although the time they take to secure these degrees does not conform to critics' expectations.

All community colleges, including urban community colleges, must address these criticisms. They must not forget their broad mission to serve their students and to remind policymakers and the public of who these students are:

- The eighteen-year-old who did well in high school and wants a marketable job skill in two years or wants to transfer to a senior college

- The student who did not do well in high school and needs a second chance
- Large numbers of adults who have seen the value of education after years in the workplace or years on public assistance
- Returning veterans
- Senior citizens who always wanted to get a degree
- Those who never benefited from reforms in precollegiate education
- Individuals seeking career changes

Urban community colleges also serve

- Newly arrived immigrants, who on a single campus often collectively speak more than fifty languages
- Large numbers of people from minority groups and historically underrepresented and underserved populations

Urban community colleges offer a first chance—and often a second chance—for their exceedingly diverse student populations. Borough of Manhattan Community College (BMCC) offers confirmation of this commitment to educational opportunity. One of the first community colleges to have a child care center integrated into its childhood education program, BMCC has plans to expand this center. Knowing that the institution can never provide enough capacity to meet the demand, college officials are now training welfare mothers to become certified child care givers in their own neighborhoods, thus providing a means of leaving welfare and improving their lives. As the contributors to *Who Cares About the Inner City? The Community College Response to Urban America* assert, urban community colleges "are viewed as the best hope for a generation of Americans that has virtually no other opportunity for education, training, and in some cases, economic and social revival" (Weindenthal, 1989, p. vii).

The purpose of the community college is to help its students achieve their goals and prepare them for their futures. Some states and cities have been wise enough to use their community colleges as vehicles for workforce development, moving people from welfare to work, building bridges to secondary school systems, and advancing students through higher levels of education. Those that fail to use the community college for workforce development will see their own economies begin to suffer.

The Issue of Access

Administering an urban community college where diverse and often underprepared student populations are increasingly the norm raises a primary challenge to access. These students frequently require remediation, exposure to technology and the information revolution, and support for future employment. Given these multiple but interrelated challenges, problems arise, as Hilary Hsu (1990) indicates, because differences in values lead to different priorities in the allocation of resources for programs and services.

Research has shown, for example, that remediation works but is costly and takes time. In virtually every study that has been conducted, students who successfully complete remediation become indistinguishable from other students (Lavin, 1996). Yet in spite of the evidence, some policymakers, in the name of standards, have made decisions to restrict or cut back these programs.

Strong public education has been the bedrock of American economic, industrial, and cultural life throughout the century. Public education has been part of the fabric of our society since the founding of the first public school in 1635. North Carolina, Georgia, Tennessee, and Vermont all established state-chartered, state-supported colleges before 1800. At the dawn of a new millennium, most states have built systems of community colleges to provide a kind of education that was not envisioned in 1635.

American ideology promotes the belief that all citizens of the United States are entitled to equal educational opportunities. Hence, colleges and universities must consider the extent to which access is being achieved. Questions regarding how economically challenged and minority students, often clustered in urban areas, attain access to college are fundamental to the goals of achieving equal educational opportunities for all students. As Muller (1996) states, "At a time when educational and political commitment to public higher education access is uncertain, urban community colleges serve as bulwarks against policies and 'master plans' that would deny underserved populations educational opportunities" (p. 59).

One of the primary discussions about access today concerns the information highway and the World Wide Web. Current decisions made by institutions and states will determine whether technology becomes a wedge that divides the advantaged from the disadvantaged or a bridge that closes opportunity gaps. But there are more pressing demands that need our leaders' attention. Technology access has become a preoccupation that has distracted political leaders from another battle concerning educational access and opportunity.

The first priority is recognizing the need to provide access to institutions of higher learning. A student has to be enrolled before any pedagogical technology can be implemented. This is the first and most obvious step toward building this country's human resources. It is increasingly clear that the future economic health of the United States rests on the shoulders of new populations, for it is their numbers that continue to grow. The past forty years of disinvestment in urban public education, the taxpayer revolts that have led to declining revenues, and the uneven distribution of public funds for education have yielded results that place the nation at a major crossroads. If choices are not made to invest in precollegiate education in cities, then the only institution that remains as a point of intervention is the urban community college.

Although remedial education has existed in American higher education since the 1870s, it is the urban community college that has taken the greatest steps to intervene on behalf of students before they reach the college's doors. A case in point is LaGuardia Community College, which has worked with at-risk youth since 1972, opening its Middle College to serve this population and two additional high schools that today exist on its campus. This strategy has become so successful that the concept has spread to twenty-nine other community colleges. Through this approach, LaGuardia's middle colleges and similar alternative high schools situated on community college campuses around the country have been able to send over 75 percent of their students on to higher education (Smith, 1998).

The Issue of Accountability

In times of limited resources, it is essential to focus on long-term goals. However, because colleges are accountable for achieving goals on a year-to-year basis, faculty and administrators must also ensure short-term achievement. Those familiar with academic life tend to believe that budget cycles come and go, bringing times of prosperity and times of difficulty. The current situation is different, however, because administrators know that they must create new ways of teaching and learning, reserve their financial resources for only those processes that add value, and adjust their expectations.

Contemporary urban community college education also faces another distraction that has moved political leaders away from a larger concern about access and also has contributed to an atmosphere of distrust in public community colleges: accountability. In business, accountability is the ability of a company to produce a good, sell it at a price that covers costs, make a reasonable return on the initial investment, and survive. Accountability is more difficult to define in the educational environment. Education is not a repetitive purchase, where the consumer learns to judge the quality and value of the service through trial and error. It is a process of development. Of course, education is a costly endeavor for the individual in terms of forgone income, and it requires a lot of time and energy. For these reasons, education is not a product in the standard business sense of the term.

The accountability challenge facing urban community colleges is remedial education, which has been under attack for quite some time. This assault has become more strident recently, as in the case of the City University of New York (see Chapter Three). Politicians, conservative commentators, and highly politicized boards of trustees are questioning whether the public should pay twice for the same thing. Such an attitude threatens access to higher education.

Some critics have assailed accountability, charging that its result is an adversarial, distrustful, regulatory, and wasteful environment. Nevertheless, community colleges must respond to accountability calls as positively and diligently as possible. Regulatory measures and political decisions and mandates will not disappear into the night.

Colleges must engage in self-study, state evaluations, progress reports, continuous institutional research, and assessment of student outcomes to highlight their achievements and challenges. The task may be tedious at times, but colleges must sincerely ask how inputs and outputs relate to each other. College administrators and faculty must open themselves to honest self-criticism.

What, for example, can be changed about teaching and learning? A willingness and courage to share good and poor results from outcome studies will strengthen institutions.

The Importance of Community

David R. Pierce (1999) recently spoke of the importance of establishing a sense of community in urban locales. Communities consist of people, government, institutions, and places of business. Urban settings present very special challenges, maintains Pierce, due to the scarcity of social and economic resources.

What, then, should the community colleges in urban America stress in their missions? First and foremost, a solid general education curriculum that includes remediation is vital. What is the body of knowledge required for a person to be a functional citizen in the urban community? Whatever the answer, it should form the general education core that urban community colleges offer. Furthermore, the curriculum should include technology. No one can be a functional citizen without having a good grasp of technology and an understanding of the role it plays in society.

Urban community colleges need to discover more ways to engage people who are at the lowest end of the economic ladder: those on welfare and those under the jurisdiction of the courts. When considering that 50 percent of black youths between the ages of eighteen and twenty-six fall into the second group, the challenge looms greatest for institutions located in settings with large African American populations.

Finally, citizenship preparation is essential. Urban community colleges have not come close to adequately preparing students to live as productive citizens in their communities. Not enough is done to impart the message to students about what a community is, how it is created, and how it functions. People create cities and institutions; if these structures are not nurtured and supported, they will collapse. Communities, and notably urban community colleges, break down and cease to function effectively when people stop cooperating.

Urban community colleges, as the chapters in this volume attest, are working to cope with conflicting forces, maintain their missions, and develop strategies that might reconcile the competing tendencies that currently typify the debate over the future and the fate of the nation's cities. By reaching out to their communities, they are serving as centers of education and instruments of social change.

References

Carter, H. M. "Student Access, Retention and Data Representation of Minorities in Urban Higher Education." Unpublished paper, New York University Center for Urban Community College Leadership, 1998.
Cheng, M. M. "Residents' Departure Tempers New York Growth." *Newsday,* Nov. 19, 1998, p. A24.
Cohen, A. M., and Brawer, F. B. *The American Community College.* (2nd ed.) San Francisco: Jossey-Bass, 1989.

Gray, W. Address to the American Association of Higher Education, Washington, D.C., 1999.

Hodgkinson, H. L. *Bringing Tomorrow into Focus*. Washington, D.C.: Institute for Educational Leadership, 1996.

Hsu, H. "The Multicultural Urban Community College: Conflict and Achievement." Paper presented at the Annual International Conference on Leadership and Development of the League for Innovation in Community Colleges, Jul. 8–10, 1990.

Jameson, F. *Postmodernism, or, the Cultural Logic of Late Capitalism*. Durham, N.C.: Duke University Press, 1991.

Lavin, D. E. *Right Versus Privilege: The Open Admissions Experiment at the City University of New York*. New York: Free Press, 1981.

Lavin, D. E. *Changing the Odds: Open Admissions and the Life Chances of the Disadvantaged*. New Haven, Conn.: Yale University Press, 1996.

Muller, G. H. "Gateways to Success: Urban Community Colleges and Administrative Diversity." In R. C. Bowen and G. H. Muller (eds.), *Achieving Administrative Diversity*. New Directions for Community Colleges, no. 94. San Francisco: Jossey-Bass, 1996.

Pierce, D. R. "The Urban Community College: A Vision for the New Century." Speech delivered at LaGuardia Community College, Mar. 24, 1999.

Richardson, R. C. "Assessing Excellence/Effectiveness in Urban Settings." Paper presented at the Annual Convention of the American Association of Community and Junior Colleges, Washington, D.C., Apr. 1–4, 1984.

Smith, J. L. Address to the LaGuardia Community College faculty, Sept. 9, 1998.

Weidenthal, M. D. *Who Cares About the Inner City? The Community College Response to Urban America*. Washington, D.C.: American Association of Community and Junior Colleges, 1989.

JOSHUA L. SMITH is director of the Center for Urban Community College Leadership at New York University.

FAYYAZ A. VELLANI is a graduate assistant at the Center for Urban Community College Leadership at New York University.

2

This chapter explores Miami-Dade Community College's internal reforms and its range of community collaborations in response to new urban challenges.

Miami-Dade Community College: Forging New Urban Partnerships

Eduardo J. Padrón, Theodore Levitt

Miami-Dade Community College opened its doors in 1960 in the midst of a momentous urban transformation. Once a haven for retirees and wintering northerners ("snowbirds"), South Florida's ultimate transformation was ensured by Cuba's revolution in 1958, which sent tens of thousands of refugees to Miami, beginning a wholesale demographic realignment there. Immigrants from throughout Central America, the Caribbean, and South America subsequently contributed to a new urban amalgam that in large part scripted the college's mission.

The early Cuban migration brought a well-educated, entrepreneurial energy to South Florida. Those skilled immigrants began the transformation of Miami from a tourist and regional service center to a hub of international trade and banking. Alongside the new economic and cultural promise, however, frustration boiled over in the African American community. The riots that shook Miami in the 1980s were born of poverty and long-standing disenfranchisement. The influx of an estimated 125,000 Mariel refugees in 1980 further congested the pool of cheap labor. Although a great deal of attention has been dedicated to healing these wounds, poverty and economic debility remain for the African American community, and in large measure for Hispanics as well, an arduous context for community growth.

The modern irony for this and so many other urban communities is that although the region's revamped economy has doubled since 1980, so too has the number of people living in poverty. In 1990 Miami-Dade County was ranked first in the nation for families living in poverty. At the center of the region, the City of Miami was the fourth poorest city nationally, with a poverty rate of 31.2 percent, and it had the lowest national median income of $16,925

(U.S. Department of Commerce, 1990). The gap between rich and poor has since widened, and, like the country as a whole, the middle class has been stretched thin.

The county population is expected to increase 35 percent by 2015, from 2.1 to 2.8 million, and the public school system enrollment will jump from 314,000 to 450,000 by 2010. In 1995, 2,500 new students per month enrolled in Miami-Dade County public schools, up from 500 per month as recently as 1989.

Forty years from the first Latin migration, Miami is approximately 50 percent Hispanic, with almost equal numbers of Anglos and African Americans. The diversity of culture, thought, and lifestyle far eclipses the catch-all labels, however, representing countries throughout Latin America and the Caribbean, and many northern areas within the United States. It is as dynamic and complex a region as any other in the country.

Miami-Dade Community College's (M-DCC) growth since 1960 has mirrored that of the region. Original enrollment numbered 1,338 credit students, housed in temporary quarters. The county is now home to a radically recast 2.1 million inhabitants. M-DCC has expanded to six campuses and several outreach centers, and its 49,800 credit students make it the largest community college in the country (Morris and Mannchen, 1998).

At its inception, the college came under the auspices of the Dade County Board of Public Instruction. In 1968, by order of the Florida legislature, community college districts were created, and district boards of trustees replaced the local school boards. Today Florida's community colleges number twenty-eight, and district boards work directly with college presidents in all matters pertaining to governance and operations. The boards, in turn, are responsible to the state board and state commissioner of education. The community college system is administered by the State Board of Community Colleges within the Florida Department of Education.

Defining the Urban Community College

South Florida's new urban mix has made M-DCC its educational home. The college hosts students from 127 countries who speak 74 languages, and it enrolls the largest number of legal aliens of any other college or university in the nation. Over 40 percent of M-DCC's students are immigrants and refugees. M-DCC has the largest enrollment in the country of African Americans as well as the largest number of Hispanics, and it awards the most associate degrees in the country to minorities.

Like the diverse community in which they live, these students bring a spirited energy to the college. They arrive fresh from high school in large numbers, but their average age, at twenty-seven, suggests a huge diversity of lifestyles, needs, and goals. All of them are breaking new ground and need specialized support.

To its credit, the community college in America has embraced underprepared students and made quality developmental work a respected element of its mission. No other institution in the country offers a more practical lifeline to the generation of at-risk minorities between ages seventeen and thirty-five. No other institution better appreciates the importance of reaching out to these people.

In Miami, the immigrant population compounds this need. Fully three-quarters of M-DCC's entering students require remedial course work in basic skills, including a large number (10 percent) who enroll in English-as-a-Second-Language (ESL) courses. Well over half of all new students at M-DCC are first-generation college students (that is, neither parent attended college).

The college's placement testing is comprehensive, and the scope and delivery of developmental courses are given great attention. In addition, the college has recently revised its entire student support system. Sensitive front-end services are essential if students are to succeed. As community colleges expand the welcome to higher education, so too do they broaden their purpose and, ultimately, the meaning of success for their students. As community colleges proceed with traditional arts and sciences curricula leading to the associate degree and baccalaureate completion, they also have recognized that one size does not fit all. As the economy proffers a host of new opportunities, the college has responded with state-of-the-art occupational programs.

Workforce Partnerships

We are in the midst of one of history's most profound periods of transformation. The simplest forms of communication are evolving; a shared time and place are no longer required. New information creates new disciplines, and new methods shape new understanding. Traditions will persist because they are enduring cornerstones of our work, but it is not a traditional world of knowledge in which we live.

Like every other enterprise today, educational institutions must pay attention to their surroundings. Yes they are typically the last to awaken, tradition bound and convinced of their audience. The circumstance in urban South Florida is made all the more pressing as the region fights for a central role in the hemisphere's economy. Beyond an image that has deterred new corporate arrivals, the matter of an underprepared workforce is a more difficult dilemma.

M-DCC recently established workforce partnerships through a wide spectrum of community projects. Its own education review was the context for more than twenty industry focus groups with faculty, students, graduates, and industry leaders. What faculty members at M-DCC teach and how they teach it drew exhaustive critique, allowing the institution to redesign where needed.

An even broader project was the restructuring of M-DCC's entire occupational program to align it with the Greater Miami Chamber of Commerce's ambitious economic development plan for the region. "One Community One Goal" is the centerpiece of the county's recent designation as a federal Empowerment Zone (EZ) by the U.S. Department of Housing and Urban Development (HUD). Such a designation carries as much as a $100 million urban development grant over ten years, to be matched by the county, and more than $200 million in tax and investment incentives (Miami-Dade County, 1998). From the beginning of this project, the college joined government and business leaders to forge a plan for job creation, the core of the EZ initiative. The cycle of poverty and violence afflicting inner-city America will not abate without such alliances.

"One Community One Goal" has identified seven target industries critical to the region's economic growth—biomedicine, film and entertainment, international commerce, education, finance, tourism, and telecommunications and information technology—and M-DCC has reorganized around them (Greater Miami Chamber of Commerce, 1997). Within these fields, over twenty new associate of science and short-term certificate programs have been developed, ranging from a physician's assistant program, with a starting wage of $57,500 annually, to air traffic controller, addiction counseling, music business, and communications technology, which combines audiovisual and computer technologies. The list must grow if the college and the region are to prosper.

The college also has taken steps to reorganize internally to make these programs more easily available to the community. Its occupational cluster concept has regrouped professional and technical programs for maximum exchange of knowledge and, more important, made programs heretofore available at only one campus now available at all the full-service campuses throughout the county. Administratively and academically, the approach has effected a more unified result for the college.

In the same direction, the college has entered a partnership with the local WAGES (Work and Gain Economic Self-Sufficiency) Coalition, Florida's welfare-to-work initiative. The college operates seven one-stop career centers throughout Miami-Dade County, offering assessment, life skills training, career counseling, job placement, and smooth transition to training programs for individuals leaving the welfare rolls.

Both of these projects reflect a new level of understanding between community and college. Without an educated workforce, the community will remain economically and socially shortsighted, bound to revisit past ills. Business and industry leaders, desperate in many cases for skilled personnel, are reaping the benefit of alliances with community colleges across the nation. National statistics indicate that a 10 percent investment in education yields more than an 8 percent increase in productivity, three times higher than the return on capital investment.

The manufacturing sector, which increasingly is shifting to computerized operations, aptly demonstrates the need. Eighty-eight percent of companies across America report difficulty in filling at least one skilled job description. One in five companies contend they cannot expand because of lack of skilled workers.

Although manufacturing may not command the economy in South Florida, the transition to an information-dominated economy is all the more pronounced in the region's emerging industries. M-DCC's continued development in occupational realms can serve as the linchpin to the economic development of the region.

Spearheaded by Vice President Albert Gore, the Clinton administration has initiated a significant investment in lifelong learning, seeking to guarantee every working American the chance to retrain for the new economy. The administration has proposed lifelong learning savings accounts, tax-free employer-funded scholarships, and a 10 percent tax credit for employers that provide educational programs in literacy, basic skills, and English. This proposal positions urban community colleges across the nation as gateways to higher education for previously disenfranchised populations (Vice President's National Summit, 1999).

Building on Tradition

Amid these changes, wisdom suggests that M-DCC remain attentive to its transfer capability and expand its horizons as well. The college's education review addressed far more than the associate of science and certificate programs. During a time when over seven hundred of M-DCC's faculty and staff teamed up to review and rework nearly every aspect of college functioning, the education review surely was the impassioned centerpiece of institutional reinvention. The influence of community input, particularly from employers who spoke about the performance of the college's students, contributed to a new balance with the more traditional social-science-oriented requirements. While applauding the technical preparation of the college's students, employers reported on their deficiency in work-related written and oral communication. This critique certainly is not surprising regarding the urban student population at M-DCC. Recent statistics on new student placement tests show that 57 percent and 72 percent of students were in need of writing and reading remedial courses, respectively. The faculty agreed to core curriculum changes for both the associate of science and associate of arts degrees that included additional English requirements and new requirements in oral expression and computer competency.

Employers also noted that M-DCC students lacked self-confidence and maturity. Although they compared favorably with university students in content and technical knowledge, they tended to lack decision-making and problem-solving skills. To address this area, the core curriculum was expanded to include a new course in reasoning, critical thinking, and ethics.

The need, however, runs deeper than a three-credit remedy. M-DCC students never have been traditional participants in academe. In fact, their presence has contributed to M-DCC's leaders developing a new understanding of higher education. The traditional notion of college in the United States led logically to an emphasis on the associate of arts degree, but guidance to students now must be more attuned to a larger evolving world. Included in M-DCC's education review was an overhaul of its student flow process, including all registration and financial aid interactions, as well as recruitment, orientation, advising, retention, and transition issues. The college has placed strong emphasis on early contact, providing students with complete information on the educational and career paths before them. Ongoing advisory contact always has been a staple of student services, but increased faculty involvement has enabled students to make wiser choices as they proceed.

A growing percentage of students are opting for the associate of science track as this degree gains respect in the new economy. In a study of Florida's fastest-growing occupations, thirty-one jobs required an associate of science degree, while only fourteen required a bachelor's degree or higher. Still, the associate of arts transfer option more than holds it own as a staple of community college education, and it too has gained the grudging respect of the university community. In Florida, a minimum of 80 percent of students entering higher education do so at a community college in accordance with the state's two-plus-two system. With regard to grade point average (GPA), Florida Department of Education statistics report that community college transfer students statewide do as well as native students in the state university system (SUS). M-DCC graduates have reaffirmed the open door policy and rebutted the critics who decry remedial education at the college level. Eighty-eight percent of all enrollees in the SUS from M-DCC maintain satisfactory GPAs, and 86 percent of those students who began in college preparatory courses at M-DCC also maintain satisfactory GPAs. Overall, one in ten students in Florida's SUS hails from M-DCC.

Although the overwhelming number of M-DCC transfer students attend institutions within the SUS, M-DCC maintains articulation agreements with fifty-one institutions nationwide. Collaborative agreements between its honors program and Smith College in Northampton, Massachusetts, and between M-DCC and Florida A&M University in Tallahassee for an engineering technology baccalaureate program are examples of ongoing special agreements.

Educating the Legislature

In Florida, full-time equivalent (FTE) funding for the SUS is double the level of funding for community colleges. The public school system also is funded at 26 percent more than community colleges. Nevertheless, following intensive efforts to affect legislation, funding increases for M-DCC finally reversed a thirty-year, 30 percent decrease in real dollar funding that lasted through 1995.

The community college system in Florida, despite national and certainly local respect, struggles to be appreciated in the state legislature. For an urban community college with high minority and immigrant enrollment, the consequences can be severe. A prime example is the trend toward performance-based funding. Although the college readily embraces the notion of improved performance, outcome measures that paint with broad strokes often miss the accomplishments of immigrant and developmental students. Rather than be punished for the nature of its student population, the college fought hard for adjustments in the outcome measures. Funding incentives now reward progress in English, basic skills development, and short-term occupational certification.

The existence of developmental courses has regularly come under fire. The latest legislative mandate forces community colleges to charge much higher tuition rates for a second try at the same developmental course. An additional piece of legislation caps the number of hours allowable for financial aid at the lowest number ever. The result is a financial inhibition for many students struggling with a new academic responsibility.

Most recently the legislature has heard a proposal from the state board of regents, the governing body for the state university system, that encroaches on the traditional community college population. The regents recommend a tiered SUS system, with lower entrance standards for several of the state's eleven universities. The proposal will increase the percentage of high school graduates admitted directly to the SUS from between 16 and 18 percent to an unprecedented 25 percent. The percentage of underprepared students will soar. Currently universities refer all students requiring additional preparation to the local community college. If the new state directive stands, the community college system will receive many of the same students it would have welcomed, only by a pointless circuitous route. And these students will depart after completing only college preparatory work.

The legislature also has requested feasibility proposals on the development of baccalaureate degree programs at four of the state's community colleges, including M-DCC. Programs in education, engineering, biomedicine, information technology, and film and entertainment are possibilities, supporting the high demand within the region. If the legislature approves the project, M-DCC conceivably could offer the baccalaureate degree as early as January 2000. For many of the college's students, who often lament the lack of personal contact in the larger university environment, the opportunity to remain in the same learning environment and continue toward a bachelor's degree will be an enormous advantage. Success rates are bound to increase as the transitional difficulties, both personal and academic, are minimized. For the faculty, the opportunity to teach more advanced courses already is generating enthusiasm.

The Influence of Technology

New information, accessibility, and, most important, new modes of learning must be explored if we are to keep pace and keep students competitive. Many urban students have no access to computers, the Internet, or distance education from their homes. M-DCC has embarked on an ambitious technology master plan, including academic programs, student support, distance education, administrative technology, and information systems. Not only must it aim to upgrade the college's systems and access consistently, but it must provide students with the means to compete. Computer courtyards, partnerships with software companies, a new core requirement in computer competency, and equipment upgrades are steps in that direction.

Faculty continue to experiment with technology in the classroom and using the Web. Many M-DCC students cannot afford the decreased personal contact that often accompanies increased use of technology, and staff and faculty remain acutely aware of that point. Their efforts to use technology to address cultural and personal learning styles are an important and necessary evolution in pedagogy.

M-DCC's distance-learning capacity has increased dramatically; it now offers forty-three courses with Internet support. Moreover, software partnerships promise enhancements that will benefit everyone—staff, faculty, and students. The college knows that how people teach and learn over the ensuing years will continue to change dramatically. Partnerships with private industry loom large in the arena.

Another brand of partnership, this one with seven community colleges across the state, has produced the new Odyssey Systems that address personnel, payroll, finance, and student tracking. This project, one of the most comprehensive systems of its kind, represents a first step in unified reporting systems for community colleges across the state.

Conclusion

The coming years will present challenges for M-DCC unlike any it has ever seen before. The South Florida demographic environment, the technological revolution, and the developing local, regional, and global economic influences combine to create a variety of enormous unknowns. One point, however, can and will remain clear: community colleges have a huge part to play in the preparation and prosperity of twenty-first-century urban America. No other institution is better positioned to provide services to such a wide range of players, including new students, private enterprise, and local and regional governments. To be successful, M-DCC must articulate a mission that remains faithful to local community development while expanding its role in contributing to regional and global economic growth. Its opportunity assessment and planning must be astute because the competition will be fierce. Proprietary institutions, private industry, and entertainment and technology giants are already encroaching on a market that was once the purview of community colleges. The collaborations created now will lay the foundation for the next phase of growth and the continued success of community college students.

References

Greater Miami Chamber of Commerce. *One Community, One Goal.* Report to the Community, 1997.

Miami-Dade County. *1998 Empowerment Zone Application/Strategic Plan.* Miami: Miami-Dade County, 1998.

Morris, C., and Mannchen, M. *Miami-Dade Community College Fact Book.* Miami: Department of Institutional Research, Miami-Dade Community College, 1998.

U.S. Department of Commerce, Census Bureau. *1990 U.S. Census Report.* Washington, D.C.: U.S. Government Printing Office, 1990.

Vice President's National Summit on Twenty-First Century Skills for Twenty-First Century Jobs [http://www.vpskillsummit.org]. Jan. 1999.

EDUARDO J. PADRÓN *is president of the Miami-Dade Community College District.*

THEODORE LEVITT *is project manager of Miami-Dade Community College's Reengineering Project and also serves as liaison for numerous college workforce partnerships.*

3

The six community colleges of the City University of New York (CUNY) differ from each other but share a common commitment to serve New York City's ever-changing population. As nontraditional institutions noted for their responsiveness to student needs, they face an uncertain future due to current contention over CUNY's open admissions policy and therefore CUNY's role as an urban public university.

CUNY's Community Colleges: Democratic Education on Trial

Joanne Reitano

The City University of New York (CUNY) epitomizes its famous urban location by being not only a vital symbol of hope and opportunity but also the perpetual target of critics and cynics. As controversial as it is ambitious, CUNY is shaped by local politics as well as national trends. Both its past history and its current plight mark its ongoing struggle to define the nature of public higher education in a democracy. CUNY's six community colleges play a central role in that quest.

Serving 200,000 students, CUNY is the nation's largest urban university and its third largest university. It consists of three types of undergraduate institutions: seven colleges granting only bachelor's degrees, four colleges granting both associate and bachelor's degrees, and six colleges granting only associate degrees. Within that framework, CUNY's community colleges have evolved into diverse, dynamic institutions that are the most democratic and multipurpose branches of public higher education in New York City. However, their function as access institutions and their status in the university are in flux today as a war is waged over how democratic CUNY should be.

Like their peer institutions across the country, CUNY's six community colleges serve three sometimes contradictory purposes: acting as a buffer for senior colleges reluctant to admit nontraditional students, providing a springboard for people seeking a second chance, and offering a safety net for those struggling to overcome educational disadvantages. Proud to be teaching institutions,

I greatly benefited from the constructive criticisms offered by Barbara Astone, Roberta Matthews, Lawrence Rushing, and particularly David Lavin, whose pioneering analyses of open admissions provide the starting point for all studies of CUNY and the basis for much of this chapter.

23

CUNY's community colleges are dedicated to addressing students' needs through new pedagogy and new programs. Ironically, the flexibility and responsiveness that are their assets also invite misunderstanding of their role as academic institutions. As a result, CUNY's community colleges reveal the strengths and weaknesses of nontraditional institutions trying to democratize the academy by serving previously underrepresented groups in unconventional ways (Dougherty, 1994; Fellows, 1970; Griffith and Connor, 1994; McGrath and Spear, 1991; Nasaw, 1979).

Traditional colleges began as liberal arts institutions that prepared young, elite, Protestant white men for the professions and political leadership. Gradually new colleges opened up to serve a variety of people, cutting across lines of class, ethnicity, gender, race, age, and disability. At the same time, the curriculum was expanded to include business, technology, applied arts, and sciences, as well as remediation. As the academy diversified, it also stratified, with the highest status reserved for the most exclusive and expensive, the most white and male-dominated liberal arts institutions.

Community colleges represented the last step in the slow process of democratizing higher education. From the start, their nontraditional functions fueled debate. As they admitted more diverse students, offered more remedial courses and career programs, adopted more innovative pedagogy, and reached out more to their communities, more questions were raised about their academic legitimacy. Yet they multiplied geometrically in response to a widespread demand for education in a country that has always considered schooling as the key to both citizenship and socioeconomic mobility. Community colleges were caught between the pluralist dream and the elitist reality of higher education in America (Dougherty, 1994; Nasaw, 1979; Reitano, 1989–1990).

This dilemma is painfully clear at CUNY today, where state and city politicians, the board of trustees, educators, the media, the clergy, civic groups, think tanks, businesspeople, students, alumni, and even some celebrities are locked in battle over access to the university (Solomon, 1998). At issue is CUNY's thirty-year-old policy of open admissions that promised a seat somewhere in the system to all students with high school diplomas or general equivalency diplomas (GEDs). Under fire is the structure of developmental education that evolved to support that policy. At risk is CUNY's identity as a public institution. Will it continue to move toward inclusion and pluralism, or will it opt for exclusion and elitism? What will be the role of the community colleges if the university is redefined? CUNY is in crisis because its fundamental commitment to democratizing higher education is in question.

Historical and Demographic Issues

CUNY draws on a long heritage of public service in a historically liberal city. In 1847 the Free Academy was established to provide higher education to "the children of the whole people." As its first president explained, "the experiment" was to see whether a high-quality "institution of learning" could be "success-fully controlled, not by the privileged few, but by the privileged many" (CUNY, 1972, p. 11). However, demand for the opportunity to learn was always curbed by admissions restrictions and the number of seats available. Over time new units were added, women and African Americans were admit-ted, and tuition-charging evening divisions were created. Still, the municipal colleges remained predominantly white, male, and middle class (Lavin and Hyllegard, 1996).

It was not until the 1950s, in response to national imperatives, that CUNY's community colleges emerged. The initial three campuses charged tuition and served white, ethnic, and middle- and working-class constituen-cies. Because space was severely limited, admissions criteria were established based on high school GPA, Scholastic Aptitude Test scores, and number of aca-demic courses taken. These institutions offered terminal technical degrees, but in keeping with the traditional origins of the junior college, they developed college-parallel curricula and saw themselves primarily as transfer institutions (Neumann, 1984).

CUNY's first three community colleges have had very different fates. In 1976, after two decades of existence, Staten Island Community College was absorbed into the new four-year College of Staten Island (CSI), which grants both associate and bachelor's degrees. Even today most of CSI's first-time freshmen are enrolled as associate degree matriculants (CUNY, 1997a). Queensborough Community College, founded in 1958, maintains the most continuity with the past. Located in a middle-class community on the fringe of suburbia, its thirty-six-acre campus includes an astronomy observatory and the Holocaust Resource Center. Of the six community colleges, it has the largest number of students under nineteen years of age, the second largest percentage of white students, and the largest proportion of students majoring in the liberal arts. The vast majority of its transfers go to nearby Queens Col-lege (CUNY, 1997a).

By comparison, Bronx Community College (BCC) has changed dramati-cally since it opened in 1957. Over some faculty opposition, its curricular emphasis shifted from the liberal arts to vocational programs just as open admissions was increasing remedial demands in the late 1970s. At the same time, the white, ethnic population was moving out of the Bronx and being replaced by people of color. Torn between their nontraditional challenges and their traditional training, the faculty scrambled to adjust (Kovar, 1996). Today BCC serves its borough through extensive precollegiate educational programs and a large language-immersion program. Its students benefit from innovative technological career options in addition to the regular academic curriculum. Despite its gracious hilltop site, BCC refuses to distance itself from the reali-ties of a changing city.

The second phase of development came in the 1960s when community colleges burgeoned nationwide. Again, different types of community colleges emerged, both in 1963. The Borough of Manhattan Community College

(BMCC) was originally designed to prepare students for employment in midtown Manhattan, but today its career programs are complemented by strong liberal arts enrollments and an outstanding math department. With more than sixteen thousand full- and part-time undergraduates, including the greatest percentage of African American students, BMCC's student body is the largest of CUNY's six community colleges (CUNY, 1997a). Capitalizing on its downtown location, BMCC has developed fruitful partnerships with the business, labor, and artistic communities of Manhattan, thereby demonstrating the limitless potential of its 4.5-acre inner-city concrete campus.

By contrast, Kingsborough Community College (KCC) sits at the edge of Brooklyn on a promontory jutting into the Atlantic Ocean. It has a beach, a boat for its marine technology program, and sixty-seven acres in a middle-class residential community. KCC enrolls a greater percentage of white students and has a higher graduation rate than any of the other five community colleges. Like Queensborough, the liberal arts and sciences attract the most majors (CUNY, 1997a, 1998a). Over the years, KCC has nurtured close academic relationships with its community and local high schools as well as with Brooklyn College.

The 1960s were a turning point for CUNY in general and its community colleges in particular. After much public pressure, admissions standards at the community colleges were relaxed in order to admit all high school students (not just those in the academic track) who graduated in the top half of their class. The College Discovery program was initiated at BCC in 1964, providing special assistance to a small number of able but poorly prepared minority students seeking a community college education. In that same year, the board of higher education extended the policy of free tuition to the community colleges, finally bringing them into the fold (Gordon, 1975). By the late 1960s, CUNY was moving toward open admissions, a policy adopted in 1969 and in dispute ever since because it was "the most ambitious effort to create educational opportunity ever attempted in American higher education" (Lavin and Hyllegard, 1996, p. 17).

Anticipating large enrollment increases, CUNY established three new community colleges. However, after a protracted struggle, Medgar Evers, located in Crown Heights, Brooklyn, became a senior college, which still grants as many certificates and associate degrees as bachelor's degrees (CUNY, 1997a). In 1968, Eugenio Maria de Hostos Community College was purposely situated in the South Bronx, a Hispanic community with the lowest per capita income in the United States. Hostos's distinctive bilingual-multicultural curriculum has always been under fire. Although still the smallest of the six community colleges, Hostos survived efforts to close it in the 1970s and criticisms that forced its president to resign in the 1990s. Thoroughly urban, Hostos's functional buildings are connected by an overpass above the Grand Concourse, a main thoroughfare, symbolizing the way in which the college itself bridges languages and cultures (CUNY, 1997a; Meyer, 1980).

The last CUNY unit, created in 1970 just as open admissions was being implemented, was Fiorello H. LaGuardia Community College, situated in a converted factory in an industrial area of Queens. The nation's first fully cooperative education community college, LaGuardia is also the only college in the country with an urban studies graduation requirement. It is proud of its learning communities, its urban archival collection, and its role in international education (Hyland, 1981; Golway, 1997; Reitano, 1997b). Like the other five units, half of LaGuardia's full-time faculty have earned doctorates, as compared to less than a fifth of community college faculty nationwide (McGrath and Spear, 1991). In sum, CUNY's community colleges evolved as six distinctive institutions over thirteen years, each one making an important contribution to a heterogeneous, dynamic city and each one endeavoring to broaden the range and reach of higher education.

A look at the demographics of CUNY's community colleges helps clarify the challenges they face. Altogether CUNY's six community colleges serve fifty-four thousand degree-seeking, credit students and eighty-three thousand non-credit students. Seventy percent are the first in their families to attend college. Averaging twenty-seven years of age, more than a third of the students support children, and two-thirds are women. Since open admissions began in 1970, CUNY's community colleges have admitted all students with high school diplomas or GEDs. In fact, over one-quarter have GEDs, and many of those with high school diplomas come from underfunded public schools where they have not had access to a college preparatory curriculum (CUNY, 1997a, 1997b). Bringing these students into college remains the most controversial component of CUNY's community college mission.

Mirroring the city itself, CUNY's community college students are racially and ethnically diverse, in contrast to community college students at the State University of New York (SUNY) or nationwide, who are predominantly white (Dougherty, 1994). The shift in national immigration policy during the 1960s had a tremendous impact on the population of New York City. Consequently, 50 percent of CUNY's community college first-time freshmen are foreign born and declare a native language other than English (CUNY, 1997a). Three CUNY units are among the nation's top twenty community colleges with the largest foreign student populations. These students are attracted to CUNY's internationally renowned ESL programs. In addition, as nonresidents, foreign students pay more tuition than residents, so the lower community college fees are important. Not all of them seek degrees (Desruisseaux, 1998).

Although demographic patterns vary by campus, CUNY's community college population in the aggregate is approximately one-third black and one-third Hispanic, with 23 percent identifying themselves as white and 11 percent as Asian (CUNY, 1997a). By comparison, minorities comprise only 22 percent of the nation's community college students (Dougherty, 1994). Currently BMCC, LaGuardia, and BCC rank second, fourth, and sixth, respectively, among the top colleges in the nation that award associate degrees to minority students. Fifth is New York City Technical College, a four-year institution that used to be a community college, has community college faculty workloads, and still gives mainly associate degrees. If these four schools were combined, CUNY would outrank first-placed Miami-Dade, which reports one figure for all of its units (LaGuardia Community College, 1998).

Because over half of CUNY's community college students come from households with an annual income of $20,000 or less, three-fifths attend school part time at some point in their college careers and are increasingly compelled to stop out for one or two terms before graduating. Half of them work full or part time while attending college (CUNY, 1997a). Although they are among the poorest community college students in the nation, they pay among the highest community college tuitions—this in a university that was free for 130 years. Funding for the community colleges is supposed to be divided evenly between the state, the city, and tuition. However, student tuition currently carries 42 percent of the budget, while the state and city consistently underpay their shares. Moreover, New York state funding for higher education has steadily declined during the 1990s while increasing nationwide. There is also a distinct disparity in state funding that favors the State University of New York over CUNY, reflecting historic upstate-downstate tensions (McCall, 1998, 1999).

The reversal of free tuition during New York City's 1976 fiscal crisis severely undercut the intent of open admissions. Student population in the university plummeted from 250,000 to 180,000. Tuition was raised twice in the next decade, imposing particular hardships on community college students, who tend to be poorer than their senior college peers. In addition, financial aid was reduced and structured in a way that hurt students whose need to work forced them to attend school part time and whose need for remediation kept them in school for more than eight semesters (Lavin and Hyllegard, 1996; Arenson, 1997). Finally, in the context of Mayor Rudolph Giuliani's welfare policies, the number of students receiving public assistance at CUNY dropped by 16,000 between 1995 and 1998 (CUNY, 1995, 1998c).

As a result of having to learn English, take developmental courses, and work and care for families, few students graduate in two years, a "failure" for which CUNY's community colleges have been repeatedly castigated by the mayor. Instead, 17 percent of CUNY's students earn an associate degree in four years, 25 percent in six years, and almost 30 percent in eight years. These graduation rates reflect national norms and do not account for students who leave in good standing or transfer before completing their degrees. In addition, nearly 40 percent of CUNY's community college students seek specific training rather than degrees (Lavin, 1997; CUNY, 1997b, 1998a).

Nontraditional in terms of socioeconomic status, academic preparation, and objectives, today's students render obsolete some of the most cherished academic conventions. The demographic profile of CUNY's community colleges reveals how democratic they have become and also suggests how complicated and politically volatile democratization can be. It requires the reassessment of assumptions about who goes to college, under what conditions, for what purposes, and for how long. It makes community colleges advocates as well as purveyors of social change.

Mission Issues

Despite their differences, CUNY's six community colleges share a common identity as gateways for students who have been traditionally underrepresented in the academy. They are multipurpose academic institutions providing remedial education, career education, liberal education, transfer preparation, and community outreach. However, at CUNY, they are not officially a system. Rather, they are part of a university comprising eleven senior colleges, six community colleges, a graduate center, and a law school. All share one board of trustees, one chancellor, and one central administrative bureaucracy.

Except for heavier faculty workloads and minimal city funding, community colleges are not formally recognized as a distinct subset in the university. They warrant no vice chancellor, no university dean, not even a special office in the central administration. Some people find this situation advantageous because it suggests that the community colleges are integral parts of the university system. Others suspect that senior college priorities drive university policy. The need for a community college voice in CUNY has found expression in the publication of a journal, *Community College Review,* the creation of the Community College Caucus within the University Faculty Senate, and the development of the grassroots CUNY Community College Conference group of faculty and staff.

CUNY's community college catalogues are bursting with courses and programs designed to meet long-standing and new labor market demands. Their students seek career training, retraining, and upgrading. Every community college has standard programs in business, computers, health, and public service. There are also unique programs, including (but hardly limited to) corporate and cable communications, electronic engineering, marine technology, nuclear medicine technology, laser and fiber optics technology, ornamental horticulture, public interest paralegal studies, respiratory therapy, travel and tourism, and veterinary technology. Some of these programs are the only ones offered in the state. None of them is really terminal because many of their students transfer or intend to pursue further education at some point in their lives.

The career programs have been criticized by scholars who claim that they "cool out" student aspirations, prevent them from transferring, track them into lower sectors of the economy, and lead to dead-end jobs (Brint and Karabel, 1989). At the other end of the spectrum are those who view the career programs as appropriate curricula for academically inferior students. Some even suggest that community colleges should not bother to teach the liberal arts and sciences at all ("Editorial: Jobs Must Jump. . . ," 1998). Both left and right reinforce the view that career education is less than legitimate education, that community colleges are vocational institutes rather than academic institutions. This perception has taken a toll on CUNY's community colleges not only in the public eye and within the university, but also in the community colleges themselves, where faculty in career programs sometimes feel like second-class citizens. Yet career education is central to the success of the community colleges, not only in terms of workforce preparation for the city and the state, but also in terms of the socioeconomic mobility of community college students (McCall, 1999; LaGuardia Community College, 1998).

The liberal arts and sciences are essential not only to the community colleges' democratic mission, but also to their students' transfer and employment prospects. As in all other colleges, these fields comprise the core of higher education, connecting each generation to the ongoing search for human meaning within a continuum of past and future. They are particularly essential for survival and social mobility in a postindustrial economy. In addition, by helping students expand the depth and breadth of their understanding of how the physical and social worlds work, the liberal arts and sciences enable students to shape and enrich their own lives. It is one of America's most extraordinary achievements that through the community colleges, this type of education has become available to so many people who were not born into the privileged classes.

Liberal arts and science programs encompass all of the traditional disciplines. In keeping with CUNY's long history of local autonomy, each college establishes its own distribution requirements. Community college faculty teach not only introductory courses but also upper-level courses that support career programs, prepare students for academic majors after transferring, or serve as electives. Liberal arts and science career programs include preeducation, communications, the fine and performing arts, allied health, human services, journalism, and preengineering. At LaGuardia, liberal arts majors take a capstone course, "Humanism, Science, and Technology," and selected students do faculty-supervised scientific research under grants from the National Aeronautics and Space Administration and the National Institutes of Health. Since 1986, the percentage of associate degrees granted in the liberal arts and sciences at the six community colleges has risen from 20 to 25 percent, moving transfer issues higher up on the university's agenda (CUNY, 1997a).

Transfer is a delicate subject at CUNY. In keeping with national trends, CUNY's community college students are much less likely to earn a bachelor's degree than students who start at senior colleges. Community college students confront difficulties in completing a bachelor's degree due to a combination of factors, including uneven support and preparation in the community colleges, insufficient financial aid, and obstacles in the senior colleges (Dougherty, 1994). This is a particularly important issue because access to baccalaureate programs through transfer was pivotal to the original vision of open admissions and remains central in student aspirations (Lavin and Hyllegard, 1996).

Although community college graduates are guaranteed the right to transfer with sixty credits within CUNY, each senior college can establish its own entrance and transfer requirements and can choose to accept community college courses as general electives rather than as exact equivalencies. Students who transfer often are required to take more remediation and pay for more than 120 credits to complete their degrees. Students in vocational programs also have to make up general education courses and may find that some specialized courses they took in the community colleges must be retaken as part of the major in the senior college (CUNY, 1993a). The extra time and expense, not to mention the frustration, of all these complications act as deterrents to completion of the bachelor's degree.

Efforts at more uniform articulation between the senior and community colleges have progressed, albeit slowly and with resistance. One strategy for bridging the divide was the creation of discipline councils to promote dialogue among faculty in similar fields across the university. They provide potential for cooperation, but the academic credibility issue still simmers beneath the surface of faculty relations. Starting with the entering class of 2000, for example, a new writing proficiency test will be required for graduation from the community colleges, transfer to the senior colleges, and progress beyond the sixtieth credit for all students. This "rising junior" exam is widely perceived as a criticism of the quality of community college education and yet another barrier to transfer.

In the meantime, several community colleges have developed honors programs to support students with small classes, initiated transfer counseling, and established membership in the national community college honors society, Phi Theta Kappa (Reitano, 1997a). Furthermore, three CUNY community colleges join four SUNY community colleges in the extremely successful Exploring Transfer program with Vassar College, a program that began as a partnership between Vassar and LaGuardia in 1985. In addition, LaGuardia has an equally successful science-oriented partnership with Barnard College. Numerous transfer agreements have been forged with local private colleges as well. The bachelor's degree completion rate of students who matriculate at Vassar, Barnard, Smith, Yale, Mount Holyoke, Wellesley, the University of Rochester, and Cornell through these programs is high (Lieberman and Hungar, 1998; Roundtree, 1995). Moreover, CUNY students accepted into New York University's Community College Transfer Opportunity Program have a 70 percent graduation rate, and many continue on to graduate school (New York University, 1999).

While the transfer issue underscores the traditional functions of CUNY's community colleges, continuing education highlights their nontraditional roles. Of course, higher education institutions have always offered concerts, plays, and guest lectures, but these have tended to be high-brow affairs. Indeed, colleges were best known for the gates and walls that separated them from their environs, not to mention the town and gown tensions they engendered. By contrast, community colleges consider themselves integral parts of the locales on which they depend for students and for financial and political support.

Consequently, they serve their communities in countless ways, performing functions and reaching out to populations never before included in the purview of college. CUNY's community colleges provide job training and career counseling for dislocated workers, displaced homemakers, welfare recipients, and the homeless. There are noncredit courses for the GED, basic skills, computer literacy, and ESL. The community is encouraged to enroll in vocational certificate programs, weekend classes for children, and personal development classes for adults. Transitional programs serve high school dropouts, veterans, and persons leaving prisons. One unit provides educational services for the homebound; another has an extensive program for the deaf. There is even a special Taxi Drivers' Institute. All units cooperate closely with labor unions, the New York City government, and local businesses to promote workplace training and economic development. In addition, the community colleges host a broad array of cultural and civic events. Hardly ivory towers, CUNY's community colleges have truly repositioned higher education in the public forum as everybody's resource for individual and collective advancement.

Contemporary Issues

Up to now, the development of CUNY's community colleges has been shaped by the system's commitment to approach gradually its original goal of serving "the whole people" (CUNY, 1972, p. 11). However, there has also been opposition to that objective from forces within CUNY, the city, and the state. Recently national and local factors have fueled the fire. Reaction against the social changes of the 1960s, coupled with mounting criticism of public educational institutions per se, and compounded by Republican victories in the state house and in city hall, set the stage for an attack on CUNY. Through their appointive powers, the mayor and the governor have created an aggressive board of trustees eager to redefine the university. Since the spring of 1997, Mayor Rudolph Giuliani has relentlessly criticized CUNY, particularly its community colleges, for having no standards. In January 1998, he declared that "open enrollment is a mistake" (Arenson, 1998a) and a year later recommended that we "blow up" the whole system (Seidman, 1997; Basinger, 1998; Giuliani, 1999).

Since then CUNY has been embroiled in an acrid debate over how democratic it should be. At issue are two key words—*remediation* and *standards*—which seem to pose a fundamental dichotomy between two other words—*access* and *excellence*. CUNY's critics contend that remediation lowers standards, is high school work, and does not belong in college, especially not in senior colleges. Its defenders claim that remediation maintains standards and legitimately provides an academic lifeline for students who are weak in some areas while strong in others, who are returning to school after several years, or who were ill served by their previous educational experiences. The question is whether access precludes excellence; it is the same question that has shadowed American higher education since its inception.

CUNY's senior colleges have always had admissions requirements, but they have also provided developmental education for students who otherwise met their entrance criteria based on high school GPA, rank in class, and SAT scores. Although remediation represents only 15.2 percent of instruction at CUNY, 51 percent of CUNY's senior college freshmen require some developmental education, which three-quarters of them typically complete in one or two semesters (CUNY, 1999b; Watson, 1997). Much concern has been raised about the cost of remediation, but CUNY data indicate that for the 1996–97 academic year, only 2.3 percent of the total operating expenditures was allotted to basic skills instruction (CUNY, 1999a).

Providing this type of transitional support to baccalaureate candidates was crucial to CUNY's open admissions policy, which was notable precisely because, with limits, it allowed open admissions students to enter every unit in the system (Lavin and Hyllegard, 1996; Nasaw, 1979). Once the board of trustees' new policy is completely phased in, students needing any developmental education will be prohibited from registering for courses in any baccalaureate program until they have passed tests marking the completion of all their remedial work in special summer institutes or at the community colleges (Arenson, 1998b). It spells the end of open admissions to bachelor's degree programs.

After months of tense, highly politicized debate, this policy was passed by a divided board of trustees in May 1998, was challenged in court, and was passed again in January 1999. A new court case initiated by several civil rights groups is under way, and the state board of regents is considering whether the remediation policy represents a fundamental change in CUNY's mission. A nonpartisan policy represents a fundamental change in CUNY's mission. A nonpartisan organization called the Friends of CUNY is bringing together concerned citizens, alumni, civic leaders, community groups, and academics to oppose the ban on remediation and to support open access. In addition, the NYC Bar Association has formed the Special Commission on the Future of CUNY, which will write a report about the public policy implications of the new remediation resolution.

During the summer of 1999, CUNY's critics consolidated their gains. Former congressman Herman Badillo, long a vociferous opponent of open admissions and Mayor Giuliani's education advisor, was appointed chairperson of the board of trustees. The position of vice chair went to Benno C. Schmidt Jr., former president of Yale and current executive director of the Edison Project, which runs public schools for profit. Schmidt has just finished leading a mayoral task force on CUNY that issued a scathing report describing a university in decline, blaming open admissions for many of its problems, supporting the elimination of remediation in the senior colleges, and recommending systemwide reorganization (Schmidt, 1999).

The report went even further, proposing that all students in CUNY should complete remediation before they enroll in college-level courses, thus converting remediation exit exams into college entrance exams. If adopted, this policy would prohibit students from entering the community colleges until they passed qualifying tests in reading, writing, and mathematics (Schmidt, 1999). It would make CUNY the first community college system in the nation to close the open door. Badillo considers the Schmidt report his blueprint for the future and has successfully recruited as CUNY's next chancellor Matthew Goldstein, the president of Adelphi University and a cautious advocate of many of the policies enunciated in the Schmidt report.

Sensitive social issues underpin the debate. Before the advent of open admissions in 1970, only 13 percent of New York City's high school graduates, most of them white and male, attended CUNY. In 1968 African Americans and Puerto Ricans accounted for almost 25 percent of New York City high school graduates but only 5 percent of CUNY's student body. Although many more whites entered CUNY through open admissions than did minorities, the new policy brought significant change. In the senior colleges, the proportion of minorities quadrupled from 4 percent to 16 percent; in the community colleges, minorities doubled from 17 percent to 33 percent. The new students tended to be economically disadvantaged, and the minority open admissions students were poorer than the white open admissions students. Economic disparities translated into academic ones because the lower-income students tended to come from weaker schools, to have been in vocational tracks, and therefore to have been less well prepared for college (Lavin and Hyllegard, 1996).

Aware of these urban realities, the board of higher education explicitly stated in its 1972 master plan that "at the heart" of CUNY's mission lay its commitment "to help break the cycle of poverty, ignorance, and discrimination—a cycle which has stifled the aspirations of a large number of the city's residents." Toward this end, it recognized the importance of providing underprepared students "with the basic skills and other special support requisite for success at the college level" (CUNY, 1972, pp. 2–4). Thus, from the start, remediation was seen as an essential tool for addressing inequities based on race, class, ethnicity, and gender. It was understood that the key to significant social change was widening access to the bachelor's degree, which is the degree most correlated with social mobility (Lavin and Hyllegard, 1996).

The defenders of remediation point out that removing it from the senior colleges will narrow the opportunities for attaining the bachelor's degree by detouring and discouraging otherwise qualified students. Currently students requiring remediation in the senior colleges graduate at almost the same rate as those not requiring remediation (Watson, 1997). Considering how many barriers to transfer already exist within the university, it is likely that the new policy will further encumber completion of the bachelor's degree.

To complicate matters, projections based on existing patterns of remediation suggest that the new policy will disproportionately harm minority students by turning away two-thirds of Asian, African American, and Hispanic freshmen, including 56 percent of female freshmen (Healy and Schmidt, 1998; Lavin and Weininger, 1998, 1999). The opponents of remediation consider these predictions extreme and patronizing to minorities, who, they insist, will meet the same standards as everyone else if those standards are made clear. The arguments mirror wider debates over affirmative action, indicating that this is not merely a local spat but rather one facet of much broader divisions over equity and opportunity and the roles of the private and public sectors in American society.

Developmental education has become the litmus test for open admissions, despite the fact that remediation was hardly a new function imposed by open admissions. Compensatory courses were provided by the original Free Academy itself and were being offered in all CUNY units prior to open admissions. A national phenomenon with a long history, remediation is so fundamental to higher education in the United States that it is offered by 81 percent of public colleges and all community colleges (Institute for Higher Education Policy, 1998).

However, the increased need for remediation after open admissions was striking to many members of the CUNY community. As early as the mid-1970s, entrance restrictions were tightened for the senior colleges, shifting more students to the community colleges. Significantly, the percentage of freshmen entering the senior colleges dropped from over half to about a third in the single year 1975–76, with the biggest decline occurring among minority students. "In terms of freshmen enrollments, then, CUNY was transformed into an institution centered around its community colleges" (Lavin and Hyllegard, 1996, p. 217).

Also in the mid-1970s, retention standards were made more stringent, and centralized skills assessment tests were instituted. Not only did students have to take more remediation, but the skills assessment tests became prerequisites for transfer to the senior colleges (Lavin and Hyllegard, 1996). Progress through the university was becoming increasingly more difficult, and the community colleges had to take remediation seriously if open admissions was to be viable.The dimensions of the task were huge. Although the numbers vary by unit and skills area, 84 to 95 percent of today's entering students take some remediation in every CUNY community college, with the majority needing at least two semesters of remediation in one or more skills areas and a third needing more than two semesters. In addition, at least a third of CUNY's community college students require two semesters of ESL, and significant numbers require more than two semesters. Many of the ESL students also need remediation (Watson, 1997; CUNY, 1997a, 1998b).

CUNY's community college faculty have met these challenges creatively and have struggled to prevent "the remedialization of the curriculum" (McGrath and Spear, 1991). They have developed new models for developmental education and ESL using computers, portfolio assessment, collaborative learning, and immersion programs. They have devised new tests, alternative assessment tools, and norming techniques. They have done studies, presented scholarly papers, written books and articles, held conferences, and published journals. They have worked with faculty in other disciplines to promote skills reinforcement across the curriculum, as well as with their senior college colleagues to build consensus and establish common standards (Anderson and others, 1983; August and Song, 1999; Gallagher, 1988; Stanley and Ambron, 1991; Trillin, 1980).

After thirty years of experience with providing extensive remedial and developmental education, CUNY's community college faculty have become recognized experts in the field. Many reject the deficit model of remediation, which emphasizes what students lack, in favor of a competency model, which builds on students' strengths in order to mainstream them into the college curriculum as quickly as possible. Using discipline-based instruction in a single course, a pair, or learning communities, teachers expose students needing remediation to college-level reading materials from standard subjects such as literature, psychology, and sociology. Studies demonstrate that students in these programs do better in their regular courses, score higher on language assessment tests, maintain higher averages, and have higher graduation rates than students in ordinary skills courses (Chaffee, 1999; Kasper, 1995–1996; Matthews and Lynch, 1997; Mlynarczyk and Babbitt, 1997).

Concerns about remediation have motivated CUNY to work more closely with the New York City high school system. In 1992 CUNY adopted the College Preparatory Initiative, which phases in a series of required high school courses that students must complete before entering CUNY or must make up while at CUNY in order to earn an associate degree. Recently New York State tightened up its regents exam requirements for high school graduation. Ideally, these changes will have long-range benefits if all schools in all neighborhoods can properly prepare all students to pass the required courses and exams. However, considering the existing inequities of New York's school system, failure to achieve that goal may increase the high school dropout rate and therefore discourage more students from pursuing their education or compel them to enter the community colleges with GEDs.

CUNY's community colleges reach out to their local schools through programs like College Now, which brings college courses to high school students. Since 1988, CUNY faculty have team-taught with high school teachers in the interdisciplinary, media-supported American Social History Project. Moreover, several of CUNY's community colleges host small alternative high schools on their campuses; LaGuardia has three, and Bronx, Kingsborough, and Hostos each have one. In-service training seminars and special sabbatical programs are also offered to public school teachers. Through these various strategies, CUNY's community colleges are building a more seamless transition between high school and college. Their efforts have expanded the conventional role of the academy and consequently have reinforced the image of community colleges as the mavericks of higher education.

Conclusion

Despite twenty years of defunding that have reduced support services, increased class size, and created a faculty dominated by adjuncts, CUNY's community colleges have remained aggressive and innovative in providing the opportunity for higher education to a broad cross-section of people in a variety of ways. However, flexibility has come at a price. Fulfilling their mission of being responsive to the city's needs has made CUNY's community colleges increasingly vulnerable to attack from within and outside academia. All too often they find themselves having to defend their integrity as academic institutions precisely because they have pursued nontraditional pedagogy and programs. Indeed, the board of trustees' new policies champion the most traditional, least flexible methods of instruction and assessment by divorcing remediation from the college curriculum and extolling testing as the ultimate measure of learning.

CUNY's community colleges confront more dilemmas than ever before, and their position in the university seems increasingly precarious. As the remediation function is shifted to their shoulders, CUNY's community colleges risk narrowing their mission accordingly. At best they may develop new partnerships with the senior colleges that will facilitate transfer; at worst they may be forced to relinquish their roles as comprehensive academic institutions. Without major budget increases and provisions for full-time faculty positions and physical expansion, community college resources will have to be shifted away from nonremedial courses. As a result, the community colleges may end up limiting their curricular offerings and underserving, or perhaps displacing, their current students in favor of bachelor's degree students whom they would not ordinarily have served at all.

CUNY's community colleges confront an identity crisis. While solidly committed to open admissions and developmental education, they want to remain multifaceted institutions, providing not just remediation but also career education, not just career education but also liberal arts education, transfer preparation, and community outreach. All of these missions are more complementary than contradictory because they are essential components of the academic whole. Together they enable community colleges to address students' varied aspirations, academic needs, and learning styles. Moreover, they provide options to nontraditional students who are doing just what college students should be doing: exploring knowledge and alternative paths to personal and professional development.

Throughout their history, CUNY's community colleges have reflected the changes affecting higher education in the United States. Like all other community colleges, they have demystified, diversified, and therefore democratized college. Their very existence affirms the proposition that all people deserve a chance, including a second chance, to seek higher education in order to participate fully in society as creative individuals, citizens, workers, leaders, and lifelong learners. The current crisis notwithstanding, CUNY's community colleges will continue trying to make this democratic ideal a reality.

References

Anderson, J. R., and others. *Integrated Skills Reinforcement: Reading, Writing, Speaking, and Listening Across the Curriculum.* New York: Longman, 1983.

Arenson, K. W. "Aid Cuts Put College Beyond Reach of Poorest Students." *New York Times,* Jan. 27, 1997, p. A16.

Arenson, K. W. "Poking Education's Sore Spot." *New York Times,* Jan. 31, 1998a, p. B3.

Arenson, K. W. "With New Admissions Policy, CUNY Steps into the Unknown." *New York Times,* May 28, 1998b, p. B3.

August, B., and Song, B. "Using Portfolios to Assess the Writing of ESL Students: A Better Standard?" Unpublished manuscript, Kingsborough Community College, City University of New York, 1999.

Basinger, J. "New York City's Mayor Calls for an End to Open Admissions at CUNY." *Chronicle of Higher Education,* Jan. 23, 1998, p. A35.

Brint, S., and Karabel, J. *The Diverted Dream: Community College and the Promise of Educational Opportunity in America, 1900–1985.* New York: Oxford University Press, 1989.

Chaffee, J. "Critical Thinking: The Cornerstone of Education." In National Center for Post-Secondary Improvement, *Remedial Education in Higher Education and the Academic Mainstream.* Palo Alto, Calif.: Stanford University Press, 1999.

City University of New York. *Master Plan of the Board of Higher Education.* New York: City University of New York, 1972.

City University of New York, Chancellor's Advisory Committee on Articulation and Transfer. *Report to the Chancellor.* New York: City University of New York, June 30, 1993a.

City University of New York, Office of Institutional Research and Analysis. "Transfer at the City University of New York: An Overview." Paper presented to the Chancellor's Advisory. New York: City University of New York, 1993b.

City University of New York, University Academic Processing Center. *Preliminary Enrollment Data Report.* New York: City University of New York, Spring 1995.

City University of New York, Office of Institutional Research and Analysis, Task Force on Articulation and Transfer. *CUNY Student Data Book I.* New York: City University of New York, Fall 1997a.

City University of New York. "Community Colleges." In *The Chancellor's Report.* New York: City University of New York, Spring 1997b.

City University of New York, Office of Institutional Research and Analysis, Task Force on Articulation and Transfer. *CUNY Student Data Book II.* New York: City University of New York, July 1998a.

City University of New York, Office of Institutional Research and Analysis. Unpublished tabulations, Chart IVB: Number of Semesters Spent in ESL and Basic Skills Courses, Fall 1996 First-Time Freshmen Entering Associate Programs, Mar. 5, 1998b.

City University of New York, University Academic Processing Center. *Preliminary Enrollment Data Report.* New York: City University of New York, Fall 1998c.

City University of New York, Budget Office. "Report on the Cost of Basic Skills Instruction and the Cost of English as a Second Language Instruction in 1996–1997." New York: City University of New York, Apr. 1999a.

City University of New York, Office of Institutional Research and Analysis. Unpublished tabulation on percentage of faculty teaching equivalents in remediation, Jan. 27, 1999b.

Desruisseaux, P. "Two-Year Colleges at Crest of Wave in U.S. Enrollment by Foreign Students." *Chronicle of Higher Education,* Dec. 11, 1998, p. A66.

Dougherty, K. J. *The Contradictory College: The Conflicting Origins, Impacts, and Futures of the Community College.* Albany: State University of New York Press, 1994.

"Editorial: Jobs Must Jump to Head of Class." *Daily News,* Feb. 23, 1998.

Fellows, G. W. "A Case Study of the Community Colleges of the City University of New York." Unpublished doctoral dissertation, Columbia University, Teachers College, 1970.

Gallagher, B. "Microcomputer Word Processing and Language Teaching: Issues, Approaches and Practical Considerations." In U.H.O. Jung (ed.), *Computers in Applied Linguistics and Language Teaching.* Frankfurt am Main: Verlag Peter Lang, 1988.

Giuliani, R. State of the City Address, Jan. 14, 1999. Available at <www.ci.nyc.ny.us>.

Golway, T. *LaGuardia Community College: The First Twenty-Five Years.* Long Island City, N.Y.: LaGuardia Community College, 1997.

Gordon, S. "The Transformation of the City University of New York, 1945–1970." Unpublished doctoral dissertation, Graduate School of Arts and Sciences, Columbia University, 1975.

Griffith, M., and Connor, A. *Democracy's Open Door: The Community College in America's Future.* Portsmouth, N.H.: Boynton/Cook, 1994.

Healy, P., and Schmidt, P. "In New York, a Standards Revolution or the Gutting of Public Colleges?" *Chronicle of Higher Education,* Jul. 10, 1998.

Hyland, J. "Change and Accommodation: Stratification Conflict in an Urban Community College." Unpublished doctoral dissertation, New School for Social Research, 1981.

Institute for Higher Education Policy. *College Remediation: What It Is, What It Costs, What's at Stake.* Washington, D.C.: Institute for Higher Education Policy, Dec. 1998.

Kasper, L. F. "Using Discipline-Based Texts to Boost College ESL Reading Instruction." *Journal of Adolescent and Adult Literacy,* 1995–1996, *39,* 298–306.

Kovar, L. C. *Here to Complete Dr. King's Dream: The Triumph and Failures of a Community College.* Lanham, Md.: University Press of America, 1996.

LaGuardia Community College, Office of Institutional Research. Division of Information Technology, *1998 Institutional Profile.* Long Island City, N.Y.: LaGuardia Community College, Sept. 1998.

Lavin, D. E. "The Past and Future of Community Colleges Under a System of Open Admissions." *Community Review,* 1997, *15,* 12–17.

Lavin, D. E., and Hyllegard, D. *Changing the Odds: Open Admissions and the Life Chances of the Disadvantaged.* Report. New Haven, Conn.: Yale University Press, 1996.

Lavin, D. E., and Weininger, E. "New Admissions Criteria at the City University of New York: Ethnic and Enrollment Consequences" and "Addendum: Their Impact on Women." Report prepared for hearings of the New York City Council, Committee on Higher Education, Mar. 19, 1998.

Lavin, D. E., and Weininger, E. "New Admissions Policy and Changing Access to CUNY's Senior and Community Colleges: What Are the Stakes?" New York: CUNY, Office of Institutional Research, 1999.

Lieberman, J. M., and Hungar, J. *Transforming Students' Lives: How "Exploring Transfer" Works and Why.* Washington, D.C.: American Association of Higher Education, 1998.

Matthews, R. S., and Lynch, D. J. "Learning Communities: Collaborative Approaches to Engaging Differences." In R. Guarasci and G. H. Cornwell (eds.), *Democratic Education in an Age of Difference: Redefining Citizenship in Higher Education.* San Francisco: Jossey-Bass, 1997.

McCall, H. C. *New York State's Higher Education Policy Vacuum.* Albany: Office of the New York State Comptroller, Sept. 1998.

McCall, H. C. *New York State's Community Colleges: Cost-Effective Engines of Educational Access and Economic Development.* Albany: Office of the New York State Comptroller, Mar. 1999.

McGrath, D., and Spear, M. B. *The Academic Crisis of the Community College.* Albany: State University of New York Press, 1991.

Meyer, G. "Hostos Community College. Its History: Continuity and Change." Unpublished report, Hostos Community College, Spring 1980.

Mlynarczyk, R., and Babbitt, M. "Campus-Based English as a Second Language Innovative Programs." Unpublished report, Kingsborough Community College, Spring 1997.

Nasaw, D. *Schooled to Order: A Social History of Public Schooling in the United States.* New York: Oxford University Press, 1979.

Neumann, F. M. "Access to Free Public Higher Education in New York City, 1847–1961." Unpublished doctoral dissertation, City University of New York, 1984.

New York University, School of Education. "Community College Transfer Opportunity Program." Unpublished report, Jan. 1999.

Reitano, J. "The Community College Mission: Access or Anarchy?" *Community Review,* 1989–1990, *10,* 5–12.

Reitano, J. "Honors Programs and the Community College Mission." *National Honors Report,* 1997a, *17,* 24–27.

Reitano, J. "LaGuardia Community College: Past and Future." Unpublished speech, LaGuardia Community College, Fall 1997b.

Roundtree, G. D. "The Evaluation of the Vassar College Exploring Transfer Program." Unpublished doctoral dissertation, Teachers College, Columbia University, 1995.

Schmidt, B. C. *The City University of New York: An Institution Adrift.* Report of the Mayor's Advisory Task Force on the City University of New York, June 7, 1999.

Seidman, D. "Rudy Takes a Paddle to CUNY." *New York Post,* Mar. 3, 1997.
Solomon, A., with Hussey, D. "Enemies of Public Education: Who Is Behind the Attacks on CUNY and SUNY?" *Village Voice,* Education Supplement, Apr. 21, 1998.
Stanley, L., and Ambron, J. (eds.). *Writing Across the Curriculum in Community Colleges.* San Francisco: Jossey-Bass, 1991.
Trillin, A., and Associates. *Teaching Basic Skills in College.* San Francisco: Jossey-Bass, 1980.
Watson, J. "CUNY Remediation/ESL Backgrounder." Report written for the CUNY Board of Trustees, Fall 1997.

JOANNE REITANO is *professor of history at LaGuardia Community College, City University of New York.*

4

Focusing on what is good for students, Seattle Central Community College exemplifies the commitment to the urban college mission that characterizes the three colleges of the Seattle system.

Seattle Community Colleges: Centered on the Urban Student

Julie Yearsley Hungar

The issue of how urban the Seattle Community Colleges should be arose during the process of deciding where to build the new buildings and locate college programs. Fortunately for the inner-city population, the timing of these decisions coincided with the heyday of the black power movement.

The system's first campus opened in 1965 in the aging buildings of Edison Technical High School, which, in its earlier incarnation as Broadway High, had once educated the city's elite. It was located in the Broadway District, between downtown and the Central District, home to most of the city's African Americans. Four years later, the college board of trustees prepared to act on the long-range plan drawn up for the system. The plan concentrated academic programs at a new campus in the northern suburbs and high-skill vocational programs at a new campus in the southwest, an urban area embracing varied neighborhoods with relatively old housing stock. The central campus was to be closed, angering Central District residents. After a heated confrontation by community activists, the trustees voted to make the central campus a third comprehensive college.

Today the Seattle Community College District is the state's largest. Three colleges—North Seattle, South Seattle, and Seattle Central—serve over forty-nine thousand students annually, including those taking state-supported, contract, and community service classes (Seppanen, 1998). Seattle Central has two satellite locations and administers the Seattle Vocational Institute, which offers basic entry-level vocational programs and basic skills courses. South Seattle operates the Duwamish Center, which provides union apprenticeship programs.

The State and City Environment

The three Seattle colleges comprise one of only two multicampus districts in the state system. The other multicampus district, in Spokane, consists of two community colleges and an extensive network of centers in the northwest region of the state. The State Board for Community and Technical Colleges directs the system and serves as a liaison between the colleges and state government. The governor appoints the state board's nine members, as well as five-member boards of trustees for each local college district. State board staff members, working with the college presidents as a group, orchestrate the submission of unified system requests to the legislature for operating and capital budgets and enrollment targets.

The state board parcels out the funds using a complex allocation formula based heavily on the number of full-time-equivalent students enrolled. Since the golden days of relatively generous state support, the community college system, along with the rest of higher education, has been losing ground in terms of funding. State colleges and universities once received 21 percent of the state's general fund; today their share is about 10 percent (Loretta Seppanen, interview, 1999).

Community and technical colleges now receive only about 56 percent of their revenue from state funds (Seppanen, 1998). Other sources of funds are tuition (18 percent), grants, contracts, student fees, and college enterprises such as bookstores. The colleges receive no local tax funds.

At the local level, Seattle's liberal political and social climate is compatible with the values of the urban community college. However, the Seattle Community Colleges have not yet developed close ties with either the political or economic power structure of the city. Dependence on state rather than local funding undoubtedly is a factor. Such lobbying as the law allows, technically restricted to providing information, naturally focuses on the state legislature as the major revenue source. Although the Seattle colleges have training contracts with many local businesses, college leaders agree on the need to develop better connections with the city's leadership as well as with many of its communities.

Another factor limiting the political and economic influence of the Seattle colleges is their location next door to the state's flagship research institution, the University of Washington (UW). In terms of recognition, political and business clout, and academic reputation, the colleges are effectively overshadowed by the UW, located a few miles north of the Central campus.

All formal political action the Seattle colleges engage in is chiefly concerned with funding and is focused at the state level. In terms of political advocacy, they have concentrated on the long-running struggle to gain state-level recognition for the needs of urban students. Involvement in local politics has consisted largely of efforts to respond to the legitimate demands of vocal community groups.

Urban Characteristics: Location, Students, Faculty, Administrators

Among the three Seattle colleges, Seattle Central is the largest. It always has been considered, and has prided itself on being, an urban campus in terms of its location and the ethnic diversity of its students. The first sentence of the Central mission statement makes this explicit: "Seattle Central Community College promotes educational excellence in a multicultural urban environment."

The college is located near what passes for a ghetto in Seattle, although as the Central District becomes gentrified, poor people are being forced to move out of the inner-city core. The main campus consists of a single five-story building, two blocks long and one block wide, with a new gymnasium and bookstore across the street. The campus is surrounded by stores, offices, apartment buildings, and an assortment of ethnic eating places.

More than half of the Central students are people of color, immigrants, and international students (Seppanen, 1998). Of those students who identify their racial or ethnic background, over 20 percent are Asian/Pacific Islander, 14 percent are African American, 10 percent are of Hispanic origin, and 1.5 percent are Native American. In addition, over five hundred international students enroll on a contract basis annually. Some 55 percent of Central students have family incomes of less than $20,000 (Seppanen, 1999); about 53 percent are first-generation college students (Bautsch, 1996).

South Seattle's campus appears much more suburban, although its arboretum offers a view of the downtown skyline a few miles to the north. Befitting its location near the headquarters of the Boeing Company, South's program emphasis has remained vocational and technical. Its image is that of a solid blue-collar institution. As recently as 1989, more than 70 percent of its students were white (Seppanen, 1990). The largest nonwhite group was Asian students, many of them immigrants and refugees in off-campus English-as-a-Second-Language (ESL) programs.

As inner-city property values have risen, the student population has changed. African Americans, Hispanic Americans, and Asian Americans, as well as immigrants and low-income Caucasians, have migrated to less costly housing in the southern and southwestern sections of the city. This area has three large housing projects, and South Seattle offers basic skills courses there. Through its ESL programs, it has developed strong ties with some of the ethnic groups concentrated in the area.

As a result of the population shift and South's outreach efforts, students of color now make up over 44 percent of South's enrollment (Seppanen, 1998). More than 21 percent are Asian Pacific Islander, 10 percent are African American, 6 percent are of Hispanic origin, and 1.6 percent are Native American. Thus, although its campus is not located in the inner city, South's student population reflects the diversity typically found in urban colleges. In fact, if the predominantly white enrollment of the Duwamish Center is taken out of the total, South is at least as diverse ethnically as Central (David Mitchell, interview, 1998).

Even at North Seattle, located amid the once all-white enclaves north of the city center, students of color have increased to 31 percent of the total (Seppanen, 1998). Fifteen percent of all students are Asian American, 6 percent are African American, 4 percent are Hispanic, and 1.2 percent are Native American. Yet the general consensus is that North, although no longer truly suburban, is not an urban campus in the same sense as its two sister colleges. A perception that North is inhospitable to students of color persists in some quarters, despite faculty and administrators' efforts to change it.

In terms of full-time faculty, Seattle Central is the most diverse campus; more than 31 percent are people of color (Maxwell, 1998). At North, the proportion is 25 percent, and at South, it is 21 percent. Central is also most diverse at the administrative level, employing 34 percent people of color, compared with 30 percent at South and 28 percent at North. Except for its first president, a Caucasian, and one person of Hispanic origin, all six of Central's presidents have been African American. Leadership at the other two campuses has always been Caucasian, except for one Asian American president at North who has since become the district chancellor. Governors' appointments to the board of trustees generally maintain balanced representation among the city's major ethnic groups.

To advocates for racial and ethnic groups who view education as a way out of poverty, the community college is a lightning rod. In Seattle, such advocates usually have made their case through pressure at the district level. Their concern is often over lack of representation in the ranks of faculty and staff. As a result, the district has developed a strong affirmative action program, usually meeting and sometimes exceeding its targets in most categories.

Academic Programs and Support Services

Each of the three campuses has a distinctive character and culture, but they share a commitment to serving urban students. Because Seattle Central has the longest history with a large and diverse population, this chapter will focus on how that campus approaches its mission.

The basic challenge is to give students what they need to succeed. Charles Mitchell, Central's president, believes that means filling in educational gaps, bolstering self-esteem, and helping to break down barriers to learning (Charles Mitchell, interview, 1998). It requires understanding and responding to the broad range of skills, goals, and cultural differences in a diverse student population. In carrying out this broad task, Central's leaders' first principle is to base every decision on what is good for students. Curricula, programs, and student services are designed to meet a wide spectrum of student needs.

Central faculty and administrators see a student-centered educational program as one that is comprehensive and academically sound. The college has a large college transfer program, with both first- and second-year courses in the humanities and the social, natural, and physical sciences. Professional and technical programs include business, nursing, biotechnology, wireless technology, culinary arts, and a cluster of communications areas: commercial art, photography, graphics, and video production. One satellite houses a wood construction program; the other is a maritime academy with a fleet of boats that prepares people for the region's marine industries.

A large basic studies division offers adult basic education and ESL courses. A separate institute prepares foreign students who have not satisfied entrance-level English proficiencies to pass the required tests. Institute students pay the full costs for their courses; no state funds are involved.

Central has a long history of serving students with disabilities, especially the deaf and hearing impaired. The college was one of four original sites for a regional federal program for the deaf. Although the federal program and funding are gone, the college still serves as a magnet for deaf and hearing-impaired students. Other colleges in the area often refer deaf students to Central, which spends $300,000 each year on interpreter services (Jan West, interview, 1998). The college also offers an interpreter training degree program and a full curriculum in American Sign Language.

To maintain a strong academic program, the college encourages risk taking and innovation, emphasizing improvement rather than penalizing mistakes. The coordinated studies program is an innovation that has paid dividends for both faculty and students. Central adapted the program from the interdisciplinary curriculum of The Evergreen State College (TESC), and it has since spread through the state community college system.

TESC, a state-supported institution founded in 1970 and located in Olympia, Washington's capital, has gained regional and national attention for its learning communities curriculum model. In 1983, with support from TESC administrators and faculty, Central faculty created the first course fashioned on the Evergreen model; now several are offered each term. Designed by faculty, they serve not only the liberal arts but also technical programs, as well as basic skills and ESL. They have proved to increase not only students' learning but also their sense of satisfaction with their college experience. Students facilitate one another's learning so that the diversity among students adds to the richness of the learning rather than serves a barrier. For faculty, teaching coordinated studies has been rejuvenating; they carry many of the learning principles back to their regular courses.

One coordinated studies cluster combines the liberal arts requirements for the college with the associate degree nursing program. The nursing program began in the 1970s with War on Poverty funding designed to give access to the health field for minorities. Central continues to maintain that function, providing extensive assistance to enable students with strong motivation but poor preparation to complete the associate degree program. The learning community aspect of the coordinated studies cluster also helps promote student retention.

Responding to student demographics, the region's reliance on international trade, and changes in society as a whole, Central includes multicultural and global learning in its list of outcomes. A multiyear Title III project in the early 1990s offered stipends to faculty in all disciplines for infusing multicultural and global learning into their courses. Not all faculty have responded, but a global education design team continues to promote expansion of multiculturalism across the curriculum.

As technology has become a significant factor in academic programs, its costs have affected college budgets. Knowing that many of their students cannot afford access to computers at home, Seattle Central administrators have committed all available funds to keeping technology up to date on campus. Large computer labs are open for students during school hours. Mathematics, writing, coordinated studies, and many technical programs also have dedicated computer labs, which are integral to their courses. Central has been offering distance-learning courses since 1984 and now offers an accredited associate of arts degree through this means. Close to fourteen hundred students enroll in distance-learning courses, using modes ranging from the Internet, CD-ROM, television, and videocassette to plain old-fashioned correspondence (Seppanen, 1998).

Reflecting a belief in the importance of student services for its urban population, Central has always budgeted more in this area than the state allocation formula provides. This has meant heavy reliance on outside funding sources. U.S. Department of Education grants, especially from Titles III and IV, have provided significant support for student services, as well as for other areas of the college. Major recent expenditures provide students automated access to registration, advising and credit card tuition payment, transcripts, grades, and information on course waiting lists.

After years of experimenting with ways to help students negotiate their initial college experience, Central has moved to mandatory advising for all new students. A stringent academic alert system tracks students for three quarters, using a series of letters and interventions to try to help them stay in school. A pilot program requires entering students who test at developmental levels to take a one-credit orientation course.

The college has a large tutoring program, which began under a Title IV grant. Initially the program was limited by the terms of the grant to serving students from the specific target population. Today collegewide tutoring is supported by a combination of annual grants from the private funds of the Seattle Central foundation and the student activities fees controlled by the student government. The service has since become a line item in the regular college budget, providing tutoring on a walk-in or appointment basis for all students.

One approach for involving urban students in campus life is an extensive program of student organizations. Over fifty organizations include clubs for every ethnic group that wishes to form one, along with clubs serving students with interests ranging from cycling to chess to Phi Theta Kappa, the community college honorary society.

College leaders believe that pride is an important contributor to academic success. They further believe that pride is fostered not only through strong academic programs and student services but also through the quality of the physical surroundings. Pursuing this principle, they have charged staff with a goal of making the campus an oasis of civility, order, and cleanliness. One element in this effort is strict enforcement of rules against fighting, drugs, and graffiti on campus. Another is attention to renovating and upgrading older facilities, keeping buildings and grounds clean and well maintained, and immediately removing graffiti.

A belief in fostering and valuing diversity is a salient feature of the college culture. Employees and students often cite diversity as one reason for choosing the college. But in 1997 campus leaders recognized that some serious issues were buried beneath a surface of peaceful coexistence. Issues included lower success rates of students of color and the lack of commitment to the multicultural curriculum among certain faculty.

To try to get beneath the surface, a committee of staff members volunteered to organize an all-college Diversity Day. Over three hundred faculty, administrators, and support staff spent the day discussing ethnic and cultural differences. An ongoing series of collegewide forums, to which students also are invited, has continued the dialogue.

School-College Collaboration

Seattle, where collaboration is a virtue, nevertheless harbors the barriers that commonly exist between educational systems. Still, there are a number of cooperative efforts across lines between the K–12 system and the colleges. One example is the Middle College High School. Modeled after the original program at LaGuardia Community College in New York, Middle College is located on Central's campus and operated by the Seattle Public Schools. Its students have already dropped out of high school or are at risk of doing so. They are expected to take the kind of responsibility for their learning that college students have, and many enroll in college classes as part of their schedule.

An example of cooperation by state mandate is Running Start. A law enacted by the state legislature enables qualified high school juniors and seniors to enroll in community college courses at no cost to the students. They may take a single class or a full course load at the college. The courses must be approved as meeting high school graduation requirements. It is possible for a student entering Running Start as a high school junior to receive both a high school diploma and an associate of arts degree two years later. Not wishing to exacerbate the city schools' enrollment decline, the Seattle colleges chose not to recruit aggressively for this program. As a result, the program has grown slowly, but Central now has over four hundred of these students (Seppanen, 1998).

Another school-college collaboration is Tech Prep, initiated by a nationwide federal grant program. Tech Prep courses are taught in the high schools by high school teachers, and students completing them earn advanced standing in community college technical programs. Teachers from the college and high schools develop curriculum for applied courses in English, mathematics, and science, as well as for foundation courses in specific technical fields. Courses are integrated into the regular high school schedule so there are no fees for enrolling. Four of Central's technical programs have Tech Prep components: business information technology, cosmetology, carpentry, and training of interpreters for the hearing impaired.

Articulation and Transfer

In the 1970s, with some prodding by the state legislature, the state's colleges and universities carved out an agreement that has given a fair amount of stability to the transfer process. All of the state's public colleges and universities, and most of the independents, subscribe to a set of common requirements for the associate of arts degree, although many of them have additional provisos. With the associate of arts degree and the requisite grade point average, students enter the baccalaureate institutions as third-year students with little or no loss of credits.

To promote transfer, Central opened a transfer center in 1990 with initial support from the Ford Foundation. University advisers come to the center for regular office hours, some on a weekly basis. Center staff encourage potential transfer students to make appointments with advisers from the institutions in which they are interested. Staff also arrange trips to nearby universities for students preparing to transfer and provide information and advice on the transfer process. The center is open to all students, but special outreach efforts are directed to students of color in an effort to increase the rate of successful transfer among these groups.

In 1994 the center compiled a report of transfer rates from spring 1990 through spring 1993 for students declaring an intent to transfer. The report showed that among students served by the center during that period, nearly 28 percent were known to have transferred to one of ten four-year institutions that provided transfer data (Roedell, 1994). The transfer rate for students from the same group who had not used the center was 16 percent. The center is now fully funded by the college, and North and South Seattle currently operate similar centers as well.

The majority of Seattle Community College students transfer to the University of Washington. In the past, the relationship between the Seattle colleges and their giant neighboring institution was primarily based on a number of small individual activities. Since 1997, joint projects involving the university and all three colleges have been started. Examples include a pilot program that enables transfer students from the Seattle colleges and three other colleges in the state to take their first year at the university in certain majors through distance learning. Collaboration with the university's evening degree program has led to the coordination of course schedules and advising, which benefits students seeking to complete associate and bachelor's degrees at night.

The relationship between Seattle Central and TESC has been close from the time the college approached Evergreen with the idea of adapting its learning communities for the two-year college. Although Evergreen is located seventy miles south of Seattle, it now draws the second largest number of transfers from Central. Strong contacts between faculty from the two institutions and students' enthusiasm for the Evergreen model have made this somewhat unlikely route attractive to many of Central's urban students.

The fruits of all these relationships and projects are the student outcomes: How many transfer, and how well do they do? The latter question has been answered definitively by three state institutions. Over a number of years, the University of Washington, Western Washington University, and Central Washington University have compared the GPAs of third-year transfers with GPAs of students who began at the baccalaureate institution. The comparative studies have found no statistically significant difference in the academic performance between these two groups (Loretta Seppanen, interview, 1999). Students who transfer from Central match the state profile.

The answer to the question of how many students transfer depends on the methodology used to determine this figure. Using the factors of the UCLA-based Transfer Assembly Project, Seattle Central's transfer rate is over 24 percent, compared with the national average of 22 percent (Seppanen, 1994). College staff believe they can do better through internal efforts as well as collaboration with the state's baccalaureate institutions.

Economic Development

For most students in technical programs, postcollege success means finding a well-paid job in their field. Seattle Central uses connections with industry to help develop and equip programs that mesh with the training needs of employers. One example is the wireless communications technology program, designed in response to local industry requests. Having forged relationships with both local and national firms, the college is now part of the Global Wireless Education Consortium, an international group of wireless companies and educational institutions collaborating to create a qualified workforce for this industry. Central is the lead institution, working with North Seattle and Bellevue community colleges, to develop skills standards for the industry. Other programs with close ties and strong support from industry include biotechnology, business information systems, and the complex of college media communications programs: graphics, design, video production, and photography.

Community Outreach

Although Seattle Central operates on the fundamental principle of serving its own students, the college does look outward to the community, largely in terms of making program-related connections with business and industry or lobbying the state legislature. Activities for the community tend to be joint projects with organizations that bring elementary and secondary school students to the campus and thus have some long-term potential for building awareness about the college.

One of these projects is the Black College Fair, held annually on campus since the early 1980s. The fair originated when members of Seattle's African American community asked a number of historically black colleges to send recruiting representatives to Seattle. Many of those making the invitation were alumni of one of these colleges, and all of them knew how successful these colleges are in educating students and producing strong role models for their community. When the colleges agreed, the organizers asked Central to host the event. Sixteen to twenty-five colleges now participate, either sending representatives or asking one of their alumni in the Seattle area to present for them. Over two thousand students, parents, and educators attend each year (Joan Ray, interview, 1999).

The college also collaborates with the Seattle chapter of Links, an African American women's service group, and the Seattle schools, to host an annual workshop for some three hundred middle school students and their parents. This event is held on campus during the college's spring break (Michelle Gherardi, interview, 1999). The day features sessions on planning and goal setting led by successful men and women from the community.

Service-learning, whereby students earn college credit for volunteer work with a variety of community organizations, is one academic program that provides community outreach. The college joined the service-learning movement early on, and by 1998, an average of three hundred students were involved in the service-learning program each year (Robert Tarpchinoff, interview, 1998).

Emerging Trends

Trends on the horizon for the Seattle colleges are, in the main, new wrinkles on current issues related to demographics, technology, entrepreneurship, workforce and welfare training, learning communities and consensus building, declining support, and concerns of the student-consumer. These issues may affect every college to some degree, but their impact on the urban college is heightened by the powerful factor of demographics.

The fundamental demographic issue is the increasing number of people of color, both native and immigrant, in urban centers relative to the white population. The white middle and upper classes still wield the economic and political power. Even as people of color and immigrants succeed in moving into the middle class, many take on the politics of their class rather than their racial or ethnic roots. What has so long been predicted for our society—that it would become a two-class system—is indeed happening, leaving urban community colleges to serve an underclass that is further distanced from society's power holders.

The growth of this two-tiered system is paralleled by the increasing conservatism and parsimony of those in power. The consequence is reduced resources for public higher education while the educational needs of students of color and nonnative speakers of English, as well as underprepared Caucasians, are growing.

Among the most pressing needs for urban students are those related to technology. Central gives high priority to funding technology, including student computer labs and classroom technology for both liberal studies and technical programs. Much of Central's technology has been paid for through such sources as fees from contract international students and grants from industry.

The move to look beyond state funding is growing as a strategy to support college programs. A 1999 retreat for Seattle Community College administrators focused heavily on the need to be entrepreneurial because legislative funds are not keeping pace with institutional demands. Costs are rising to meet technological change and expansion, growing numbers of basic education and ESL students, and the rising expectations of the student-as-consumer and of business and industry for a better-trained workforce.

Entrepreneurship will increase Central's external focus out of necessity. Partnerships with business and industry will be a key to keeping technical programs current and identifying new programs as a need for them emerges. The college also needs the support of the business lobby to keep special legislative funding for workforce training. Connections with organized labor, which had been limited, are becoming more important as unions insist on a larger role in planning for workforce training.

At the same time, the college must look inward and find creative ways to respond to legislators' and employers' demands for rapid and relevant training. Students too are shopping for programs and courses that are convenient and most likely to lead to a job paying a living wage. At least 20 percent of Central's students already have a bachelor's degree. In Seattle and nearby suburbs, they can choose from Central, its two sister colleges, six other community colleges, and two technical colleges. This puts pressure on Seattle's colleges to develop new programs attractive to students and to take good care of the students when they come.

Retention is not a new issue, but given the competition, it is emerging as more crucial than ever before. Retention is important not only for institutional survival, but also for increasing the success of nontraditional students. A state board research study found that the transfer rate of students who completed at least eighteen quarter credits and the first college-level math course was 48 percent, compared to 13 percent for all students (Seppanen, 1994). Furthermore, African American, Native American, and Hispanic students all transferred at rates below the average. Clearly urban institutions must find more effective means of keeping these students progressing in college.

One significant trend in taking care of students is the growth of learning communities. Research on Seattle Central's coordinated studies courses shows that they excel at retaining students for the duration of the course, bettering the 80 percent average retention rate of all courses by ten percentage points. Although students in these courses are no more likely than others to continue from one term to the next, the concept could be instructive in designing retention strategies. Relationships with faculty and involvement in the learning process are key to student success, and coordinated studies courses provide a high measure of both.

An issue of continuing concern is the task of finding the right faculty to teach urban community college students. One facet of this issue is the search for educated people of color willing to make the financial sacrifice that teaching often entails. Seattle Central and its sister colleges view this as a continuing effort. A small but heartening trend is the number of professionals who are looking for the satisfactions of a teaching career and are attracted precisely by the diversity of Central's students and staff.

Whatever their race or ethnicity, effective faculty today need to be able to satisfy the expectations of the student-consumer. Faculty must be responsive and open, technologically literate, academically challenging, and lively. Another trend is the increasing attention to faculty development, an old concept but one that is receiving fresh attention. At Central, this has taken the form of enriched support for curricular innovation and participation in regional and national projects and programs. In addition, most administrators recognize that they must be consensus builders to support motivated and creative faculty.

Policy Issues

Chiefly state-level policy is of concern to Washington community colleges. Except for city policy affecting building and expansion plans, Seattle's city government has little to do with the colleges. At the state level, the main policy issues revolve around funding. The legislature sets tuition and fees, acting on recommendations from the Higher Education Coordinating Board. The baccalaureate institutions are lobbying the legislature to allow them to set their own tuition as a means of controlling revenue. The community college system would prefer not to be included in this policy change, which could potentially foment damaging competition among colleges. The solution, should the legislature allow the colleges to set tuition, would be to have all community college tuition set at the state board level.

The state also largely controls salary increases. Equity for part-time instructors has resurfaced as a heated issue, and legislators have made some improvement in part-time pay. It is not enough to satisfy disaffected part-timers, though, and they are exerting continuing pressure to provide increases from the small discretionary funds in local district budgets.

The policy that determines funding allocations for basic skills and ESL courses is a state board–level issue that is critical not only to Seattle Central but to South, North, and a small number of other colleges with large immigrant populations. A majority of the state's colleges would benefit from a shift in the allocation model that would reduce funding for these programs. The Seattle district and the other colleges that would be affected by such changes are working together to maintain support for the current model.

Conclusion

All three of the Seattle Community Colleges bring to their mission a commitment to serve students. Although Central is most commonly viewed as the inner-city school and has been in that role for the longest period, its sister colleges in the district face similar challenges: to reach out to provide opportunities for people who choose to attend them for a variety of personal reasons, among them dropping out of school and trying a comeback, attending a college close to home, not being able to meet the requirements of a university, having graduated from a university and needing job skills, or simply needing the kind of support that a community college can give.

Urban students present special challenges in both degree and kind. More likely to be poor, to be a member of a racial or ethnic minority, to be a first-generation college student, and to have family responsibilities, these students need extra support to stay afloat in college. Their needs, which have never before been greater, call for greater effort from the Seattle colleges and their partners in urban education. These colleges have the power to reduce the growing separation of American society that is based on economic class and ethnic identity. They are more than ever a major path to equality.

References

Bautsch, J. "Low-Income Students at South Central Community College." Unpublished report, Seattle Central Community College Planning and Research Office, 1996.

Maxwell, B. "Seattle Central Community College District Student Data." Unpublished report, Seattle Community College District Research Office, 1998.

Roedell, M. "Annual Report of the Seattle Central Community College Transfer Center." Unpublished report, Seattle Central Community College Transfer Center, 1994.

Seppanen, L. *Academic Year Report 1988–89.* Olympia, Wash.: State Board for Community College Education, 1990.

Seppanen, L. *Transfer Outcomes in Washington Community Colleges.* Olympia, Wash.: State Board for Community and Technical Colleges, 1994.

Seppanen, L. *Academic Year Report 1997–98.* Olympia, Wash.: State Board for Community and Technical Colleges, 1998.

Seppanen, L. "Income Status, Seattle Central Community College District Students," memorandum, Washington State Board for Community and Technical Colleges, Mar. 1, 1999.

JULIE YEARSLEY HUNGAR is vice chancellor emeritus of the Seattle Community Colleges and was a faculty member and administrator at Seattle Central Community College.

5

This case study of the Los Angeles Community Colleges presents the challenges of a district that is trying to cope with changing social and economic needs.

The Los Angeles Community Colleges: Pathways to Urban Change

Jack Fujimoto

Los Angeles is often compared to New York City because, like Ellis Island, Los Angeles is the focal point for congregating immigrants, mainly from the Pacific Rim and countries south of the border. According to the 1990 census, 3 million foreign-born individuals reside in Los Angeles County. This represents 45 percent of the immigrants in the state of California and 15 percent of all immigrants in the United States. Of considerable importance to the Los Angeles Community College District (LACCD) and its nine colleges is the fact that two-thirds of all immigrants in the county live in the district's educational service area.

The changing demographics in the LACCD service area pose societal and economic issues that need to be addressed from an educational perspective. If gateways to democracy are to be open for immigrants as well as natives, and if these opportunities are to be effective in helping the new arrivals to become knowledgeable citizens and voters, LACCD can and should play a major role.

LACCD and other large metropolitan urban educational centers that have conflicting needs face a number of challenges. Analyzing these challenges through the lens of conflicting values theory, which attempts to reconcile the disparate educational functions with the needs of a society and an economy, has resulted in some progress, but these efforts need to be expanded.

Within Los Angeles County, rapidly changing demographics exacerbate the situation. For LACCD, it must act as a political change agent for its large urban constituency, while simultaneously serving as an educational change agent for those wanting to transfer to a university and for those looking to obtain occupational and skills certification, personal improvement, or language skills development.

NEW DIRECTIONS FOR COMMUNITY COLLEGES, no. 107, Fall 1999   © Jossey-Bass Publishers

LACCD's burden is compounded by the fact that 20 percent of the potential students from its service area—1 million people—have limited proficiency in the English language. Even the twelve suburban community colleges that surround the LACCD serve a population that is 11 percent limited English proficient (LEP). In comparison, only 9.5 percent of the state of California's population is LEP, as is 3 percent of the nation's. These figures make it clear that the need for English-language training in the County of Los Angeles exists primarily in the urban LACCD institutions (Office of Research and Planning, 1998).

Along with the high immigrant and LEP populations is another demographic trend that needs to be considered as the conflicting values theory is used to analyze the local situation. A study by the Chancellor's Office of the California Community Colleges projects a "Tidal Wave II" of new incoming students to California's 107 community colleges. By the year 2005, approximately 450,000 students will need access to these colleges if a participation rate of 7.8 percent is assumed (California Community Colleges, 1998). This means that LACCD should provide access to, and have the capacity to accommodate, 350,000 students (based on 5 million residents), compared to a 1997 enrollment of 103,000 students. The implications of accommodating a twofold increase in student numbers in less than ten years are formidable, and the likelihood of accomplishing this feat by 2005 is low, if not impossible.

The variety of challenges that LACCD faces—Tidal Wave II, the dynamic demographic mix, a large LEP population, and an increasing recent immigrant population—needs to be considered not only in terms of providing educational services, but also in terms of meeting the economic and civic needs of all residents in the district service area. The colleges' missions and resources need to be taken into account in deciding how to prioritize the needs and how to respond to these challenges.

Historical Perspective

Prior to 1969, the Los Angeles community colleges were part of the city's elementary and secondary school systems. They functioned as the higher education division of the Los Angeles Unified School District and were supervised by a superintendent, who reported to an elected board of education. On July 1, 1969, the LACCD opened with eight geographically connected but culturally and economically diverse colleges. Today nine colleges comprise the LACCD system.

In 1929, Los Angeles City College was opened at the foot of the Griffith Observatory in the Santa Monica Mountains. Its campus temporarily housed the University of California at Los Angeles (UCLA), prior to its move to Westwood. The campus also served as the starting point for what is known today as California State University at Los Angeles. Today Los Angeles City College features a mix of diverse cultures, including students from Korea, Armenia, the Middle East, India, Latin America, and Eastern Europe. Its campus, near downtown Los Angeles, is surrounded by a concentration of hospitals, film studios, and religious organizations. Taking advantage of its proximity to Hollywood, it has emphasized the media arts and radio and television production, as well as theater.

The many returning military personnel seeking higher education immediately after World War II signaled the need for more junior colleges in Los Angeles. In 1945, the board of education established East Los Angeles College (East), which spans several municipalities. For many years, the Hispanic population was dominant. More recently, Asian immigrants have moved to East's service area to establish a new upscale Chinatown, akin to an Asian Beverly Hills. Today East serves an ethnically and culturally diverse area.

In 1947, the Pierce College of Agriculture was opened on four hundred acres of open land in the western end of the San Fernando Valley. The college was named for Clarence Pierce, president of the board of education at the time but better known for the Pierce family chain of mortuaries. Today Pierce College serves several large suburban communities. Although its name features agriculture, the current campus is located in an urban jungle dominated by several high-rise buildings. The college service area includes a strong economic base of biotechnology, electronics, health maintenance organizations, and aerospace. Several major Fortune 500 corporate headquarters are located in the San Fernando Valley.

In 1949, Los Angeles Valley College, located in the eastern end of the San Fernando Valley, was opened. It serves large bedroom communities on the north side of the Santa Monica Mountains, the same mountains that feature City College on its south side. Today Valley College is in the center of a growing multimedia and entertainment industry. A local airport, as well as NBC, Disney, and Universal Studios, offer strong bases for economic development. The communities in this service area are also showing dynamic shifts in ethnicity, exemplified by a highly visible Thai *wat* (temple). Valley College pioneered the concept of educational learning centers in community colleges, having opened its Basic Skills Laboratory in 1965. Today learning resource centers can be found on most major campuses.

In the same year, 1949, Los Angeles Harbor College opened in the cities bordering Los Angeles Harbor and the Pacific Ocean. Its communities feature a sizable Pacific Islander immigrant group, primarily from Samoa and Tonga. Throughout its existence, Harbor College has maintained a steady student enrollment of eight thousand.

In 1950, Los Angeles Trade-Technical College and Los Angeles Metropolitan College opened in the plant of the Frank Wiggins Trade School in the core of the inner city. One portion was dedicated to the trades, and the other was used primarily for business skill development. Trade Tech was the premier institution for the trades and technical and industrial preparation, and students enrolled there for both job preparation and continuing education. In later years, LACCD collapsed the Metropolitan College into Trade Tech, thereby making it more of a comprehensive college. Today half of its course offerings are in the nontrades areas.

In 1967, Los Angeles Southwest College was opened in response to the racially based Watts riots of 1965. Residents of South Central Los Angeles needed educational opportunities, and affirmative action programs mandated that they would be offered. The college provided an opportunity for upward mobility for African Americans. Southwest was a highly experimental institution, willing to try out new ideas in educational theory. One of its more successful experiments was its middle college project, a venture with local high schools to place disadvantaged students in a college environment. The Ford Foundation supported programs to increase student transfers among the predominantly black student population. Today the ethnicity of students at Southwest is increasingly Hispanic.

In 1969, just prior to the formation of LACCD, West Los Angeles College was opened. Its first class was held in the Culver City public jailhouse. Ten years later, West developed the Airport College Center at Los Angeles International Airport. It had more than five hundred students enrolled in aviation mechanics and aviation electronics, vital to keeping commercial and private aircraft maintained and safe. Political squabbles have inhibited West's growth. Neither neighboring colleges, such as UCLA and Santa Monica College, nor competitors, such as the Northrop School of Aviation, have allowed for expansion, and disagreements have arisen between Culver City and the County of Los Angeles, and among the colleges within the LACCD system.

In 1969, at the time of the breakaway from the Los Angeles Unified School District, LACCD had co-terminus boundaries with the district. It later expanded its service areas to include numerous additional communities, bringing it to today's 882-square-mile service area.

In 1975, Mission College, the ninth college, opened. Controversy surrounded its opening; some thought that it should be a branch campus of Valley or Pierce College, and others wanted it to be independent in providing educational services to a socially and economically poor section of the San Fernando Valley. It began as a storefront college, offering courses in eighty-four locations at one time, including retail establishments and even neighborhood bars. In 1990, a permanent campus was built on twenty-two acres in Sylmar. The dramatic decrease from four hundred acres for Pierce College to twenty-two acres for Mission College illustrates the increasing cost of real estate in the San Fernando Valley over the past fifty years. Today Mission College has one of the most modern learning resources centers to serve its student population, which is more than 60 percent Hispanic, and still socially and economically struggling.

The logo of LACCD features ten leaves on one primary stem, topped by the main leaf. Although there are only nine colleges, the tenth represents the outreach colleges. For example, Metropolitan College was resurrected to serve primarily U.S. armed services personnel stationed in Europe, East Asia, and isolated stations such as Diego Garcia Island in the Indian Ocean and Guantanamo Bay in Cuba. Metropolitan College once again folded its operations after a four-year life, but the legacy of that experience is still carried on many transcripts.

Each of the nine colleges in the LACCD system has a unique story. Pierce College and West Los Angeles College have even been the subjects of doctoral dissertations. For this chapter, the focus is on LACCD as a system, and the intent is to provide guidance to community college leaders engaged in developing policies to meet diverse educational missions. The process is challenging, because some of the colleges (Pierce, Valley, Harbor, and West) have strong economic bases, while others (Southwest, Mission, East, Trade Tech, and City) have high immigrant rates and weak economic bases. The latter institutions, except Mission, represent the bulk of the inner core of the City of Los Angeles. Policies should provide stability to the system in terms of physical, human, and fiscal resources and, at the same time, encourage the creation of educational programs that meet the needs of its students and improve the social and economic conditions of their communities.

Enrollment

The 1960 Master Plan for Higher Education in California put some constraints on the eligibility of high school graduating seniors to qualify for entry into the University of California (limited to the top one-eighth) and the California State Universities (limited to the top one-third). All graduating seniors were eligible to go to the community college in their district at that time. Therefore, for two-thirds of the students, one of the 107 California community colleges was their only option for public higher education in the state.

At the time the master plan was passed by the legislature, the colleges in Los Angeles were still part of the Los Angeles Unified School District. As a result, there could be a relatively smooth transfer of students from their senior year in high school to freshman year in the junior colleges. This continuity provided an easy transition between the systems, but it also resulted in the belief that the junior college experience was merely an extension of, or even more of the same as, high school.

Despite these doubts about the quality of the learning experience offered by the junior colleges, LACCD enrollments began to increase dramatically, starting in 1969, and soon exceeded enrollments in the adult schools of the Los Angeles Unified School District. The addition of colleges to the system was an attempt to increase the enrollment capacity. Junior college enrollment peaked at 139,000 in 1981. Enrollment declined to a low of 93,000 in 1985 and began slowly climbing again, reaching 103,000 in 1997 (Office of Instruction and Student Services, 1999). Enrollment counts are critical to community colleges because they determine state funding. Unfortunately, only credit enrollment is reported for state reimbursement. Not included are the many students who enroll in community education and community services classes, or noncredit, citizenship, special adult education, and economic development programs.

Between 1969 and 1997, enrollments became more difficult to project and therefore were less of a barometer for college budget allocations. This is partially attributed to the "free-flow" issue, which in 1987 opened the gates for students in California to go to any community college in the state. Until that time, students in the LACCD service area virtually lobbied for permits to attend another college outside the district. The usual reason given was that programs or courses were unavailable in LACCD. However, because of the district's database of three thousand courses, such exemptions were rarely granted.

As a result of the free-flow policy, LACCD lost students to neighboring suburban community colleges. Common reasons cited by students for attending institutions outside LACCD were the better facilities and higher transfer rates of these colleges. During the 1990s, the net outflow of students from the LACCD service area averaged 40,000 annually, a sizable revenue base that LACCD has lost. This issue needs to be addressed because LACCD will be teaching those who have less mobility, less income, and fewer opportunities.

Further inhibiting the ability of the colleges to maximize enrollments is the existence of California's complex accounting system and reimbursement processes, which are often revised through the end of the state's legislative session in October. Under these circumstances, codification of legislation becomes effective January 1 of the following year. However, academic planners have printed schedules and enrollment figures by December. This mismatch of key decision dates between the state and institutions causes considerable dilemmas for college administrators.

Two examples come to mind. In 1983, the state allocation to community colleges was cut by $30 million, with implementation effective in January. A "last in, first out" method was chosen to eliminate courses in order to save costs. In LACCD, courses in real estate and martial arts, two popular programs, were canceled, and students were deenrolled, being added to other class sections if openings existed or dropped. The net result was chaos and a further reduction in enrollment.

In 1993, a fifty-dollar differential fee was assessed for each credit unit that a baccalaureate degree holder took. Once again, many students did not return to college and asked for refunds. Once again, the net result was chaos and a further drop in enrollment.

Enrollment management was also complicated by a legal decision that required immigrants to show proof of residency. Without such evidence, students were considered to be out-of-state or foreign students, and they were charged the higher rate of $120 per unit rather than the residents' rate of $5 per unit.

It is also interesting to note that the California state auditor chided the LACCD colleges for the poor condition of their facilities, which also affects students' decisions to enroll at their campuses (California State Auditor, 1998). A modernization of facilities needs to be undertaken in order to compete with neighboring community colleges.

Student Diversity

The LACCD student profile for 1997 shows considerable diversity. These data can serve as a source of educational change in LACCD. Sixty percent of LACCD students are females. Fifty percent are below the age of twenty-five. Within this younger population, large numbers are female, Asian, and Hispanic.

Overall, Hispanics comprise 42 percent; whites, 21 percent; blacks, 17 percent; and Asians, 14 percent. Especially noteworthy is the two-to-one ratio of black females to males. Also interesting is the high "undecided" rate (17 percent) among Hispanics about their college goals. Whites are the dominant group seeking occupational education and personal development programs, certificates, and associate degrees. Asians are clearly focused on transfer.

Ninety percent live within district boundaries, and 3 percent are international students. However, this high percentage of in-district students disguises the fact that many district residents are choosing to attend colleges outside the LACCD system.

In terms of academic preparation, 65 percent of the incoming students have high school diplomas, and 5 percent have advanced, postassociate-level degrees. With 35 percent needing high school diplomas, the LACCD colleges should offer courses for the general equivalency diploma. This is an area in which collaboration with high schools and adult schools could contribute immensely to the educational process.

Students are equally distributed among those enrolled as day-only students (42 percent), evening-only students (36 percent), and both (22 percent). Typically, full-time instructors are available for day-only students. In recognition of the distribution of students, LACCD might want to evaluate the costs and benefits of hiring full-time instructors for evening classes.

Thirty-six percent took a full load of twelve hours or more, with remaining students split evenly between fewer than six hours and between six and twelve hours. Since enrollments are the primary source of revenue, LACCD should increase its revenue stream by counseling students to take additional courses.

Thirty-six percent indicated academic transfer as their educational objective, with 36 percent marking work preparation or job skill development, 14 percent personal development courses, and 14 percent undecided. Hispanic students are more likely than members of other ethnic groups to be undecided about their educational objectives.

The diversity of the students should be taken into account in developing schedules of classes that increase participation rates for all groups. It appears to be an opportune time for LACCD leadership to address several issues, including increasing enrollment capacity to accommodate Tidal Wave II, serving a diverse student population, using findings from research, and improving its revenue base through a balance of student outflow and inflow (California Citizens Commission on Higher Education, 1998).

Leadership for Institutional Stability

Over the past few years, the LACCD leadership has shown a lack of commitment to governing the system of colleges in a way that promotes institutional stability.

Erickson (1997), in his detailed study of the LACCD crises of 1981 and 1987, credits strong leadership with keeping the colleges open and the district functioning. He describes the crises in terms of students whose schedules are compromised because of a shortage of classes brought on by fiscal constraints; who are dissatisfied with inadequate facilities and equipment, and lack of staff commitment for counseling, financial assistance, and individualized tutoring sessions; and whose academic needs are being met by neighboring colleges.

Erickson describes the impact of unions on the governance and fiscal situation within LACCD, their fight to control the policymakers (trustees) and prevent layoffs, while securing salary increases through strike threats. Eventually the unions prevailed in 1989 with a large salary increase, which was followed in 1997 by another large salary increase that the chancellor did not recommend but the trustees enacted nevertheless. The chancellor resigned soon after. Later, this salary raise became the focus of the California state auditor's charge to the district to address its "costly decisions."

In any event, according to Erickson, strong leadership preserved the district and allowed it to fulfill its mission of providing educational services to its public. The leadership was stable until the faculty layoffs of 1986, when the chancellor reorganized the district's administrative cadre.

Between 1987 and 1998, the district had three permanent chancellors and three interim chancellors. It was once again in crisis, facing a budget deficit, enrollment problems, decentralization pressures, and labor contract negotiations. Although district leadership was unstable, the same could be said of the union leadership. The American Federation of Teachers had its fourth president in the decade. Even the board of trustees changed every two years.

It is encouraging to note that the board of trustees adopted policies in 1998 to undertake a decentralization process that will vest more decision-making authority in the college presidents. Although these reforms were initiated in response to the district's fiscal problems, the California state auditor does not believe that these reforms adequately address the costly decisions and poor budgeting practices that contributed to the financial problems.

The decentralization process creates a new set of challenges that LACCD must address amid its current fiscal difficulties. Accountability needs to be clarified, codified, and enforced through defined roles and responsibilities as the burden shifts from the central office to the colleges (California State Auditor, 1998).

When the original board of trustees was seated in 1969, some thirty years ago, it was considered to be a springboard for higher elective office. Trustee Edmund G. Brown eventually became governor of California and a national presidential candidate. Several others from that same board were elected to the California State legislature. This process continues; former trustees were elected to the California State Assembly in 1996 and 1998. Although trustees are not expected to make lifetime commitments to these positions, there is no place in the system for individuals who seek the position primarily as a stepping-stone to higher office. What is needed instead is a commitment to the decentralization process that can lead to each campus's balancing its budgets, as well as becoming more competitive and creative in meeting the educational needs of its constituents.

Fiscal Health

The LACCD crisis was triggered by the 1978 passage of voter-initiated Proposition 13, which reduced local tax revenues to such an extent that community college funding was shifted to the state. To that end, the California State lottery provided one-third of its funds to the education sector that the community colleges shared with the K–12 public sector. Public education was guaranteed 40 percent of the state's budget. Of that amount, the community college share has been between 9 and 10.5 percent.

The colleges themselves tried to address the fiscal crises in a variety of ways. Between 1991 and 1993, student fees were increased from five dollars to ten dollars per unit. A differential fee of fifty dollars per unit was assessed for those holding a baccalaureate or higher degree. Local parking and health fees were mandated. Instructional materials fees were imposed in many instances. Courses, which needed to be recertified through the Chancellor's Office of the California Community Colleges in order to qualify for state allocations, were analyzed by college curriculum committees and revised to ensure their relevance to a certificate or associate degree program. As a result of these measures, many students were discouraged from attending community colleges, and statewide enrollment decreased from 1.5 million to 1.2 million. The Northridge earthquake of January 17, 1994, exacerbated an already deteriorating enrollment and financial situation. Chancellor Neil Yoneji (1996) described fiscal year 1993–94 as one of the worst years in LACCD history.

Yoneji, who became permanent chancellor for LACCD in 1994, recognized that the colleges were unable to offer the most appropriate mix of classes to meet current and changing student demands and that a disproportionate amount of funds was being earmarked for noninstructional and nonstudent services programs. He embarked on a four-point program, starting with a faculty retirement plan in November 1994. More than 250 faculty retired, resulting in a reallocation of funds to needed programs.

Next was a strategy for reorganizing the district to reduce noninstructional costs. In April 1995, a retirement incentive was provided to administrators, prompting fifteen to leave the ranks. There was considerable clamor for such an incentive to be offered to support staff; however, it never occurred.

The third strategy was to expand educational opportunities through collaboration and partnerships with other educational institutions, nonprofit organizations, the private sector, and the public. These are not high-cost items but a means of articulating concerns with like-minded professionals.

The fourth and last strategy that Yoneji proposed was a comprehensive review of educational programs. This was definitely needed when 1998 data from the LACCD Research Office showed that the productivity index for LACCD classes is considerably lower than the statewide average (Office of Research and Planning, 1998).

Collaborations and Partnerships

Between 1988 and 1998, LACCD played a significant role in implementing the federally mandated Immigration Reform Control Act (IRCA) of 1986, which contributed significantly to the fiscal health of several colleges. Initially the process of sorting out "eligibles" from undocumented "illegals" or post-1982 documented immigrants was difficult.

LACCD worked in partnership with the Los Angeles Unified School District to develop a system that assessed English-language and civics competencies, along with instruction necessary to meet federal guidelines imposed by the Immigration and Naturalization Service. This was a tremendous undertaking. In the first year, the combined entities stated that more than 400,000 immigrants in Los Angeles County were served through outreach, counseling, assessment, and instruction (Fujimoto, 1992).

Collaborative activities for sharing program information and curricula were initiated with community-based agencies such as La Hermanidad Mexicana, One Stop Immigration, and Catholic Charities, along with nonprofit coalitions such as Los Angeles County Collaborative for Amnesty. This was later expanded to become California Community College Educators of New Californians.

The continuing political and leadership issues, combined with the fiscal problems, precluded the apportionment of resources to meet such social needs (Erickson, 1997). However, the curriculum controversy over English-language acquisition was debated and studied by faculty teaching English-language preparatory courses as well as ESL courses. The English Language Institute was formed to determine hours of instruction, number of units for each course, articulation of courses, and impact on faculty workloads.

One formidable obstacle to successful implementation of IRCA was the need to create a way to reimburse those who were providing instructional services to amnesty program eligibles. Working through coalitions to develop collaborative programs of assessment, curriculum, record maintenance, and apportionment was a learning experience. Working collaboratively for legislation to provide funding to all amnesty programs, especially in Los Angeles and Orange counties where the bulk of that population resided, was a major undertaking. Guiding the state bureaucracies, as well as local public and private schools, parochial structures, and community-based organizations, was time-consuming and fraught with misunderstandings based on perception, awareness levels, sensitivity, training, and the effects of duplication of effort in amnesty programs.

The amnesty and citizenship programs brought federal funds to colleges in LACCD. Most colleges used these additional funds to balance their potential or actual deficits. One of the valuable lessons from this decade of experience with the amnesty and citizenship programs was that LACCD had difficulty institutionalizing these types of social programs into its cultural fabric. This was also true in economic development and contract education programs (Fujimoto, 1994). However, providing educational services for social programs is much different and more difficult than for an economic development program for training or retraining of employees where rules are clearly defined.

What Is the Future?

As an urban community college with a large foreign-born and LEP base, LACCD should undertake a dedicated and committed process to change. Decentralization has been selected as the direction. The AFT Faculty Taskforce on Reform and Decentralization published a decentralization model that contains short-term planning guides to restructure the district (AFT Faculty Guild, 1998). Further research on the issues of enrollment, diversity, institutional stability, and fiscal integrity should help in the decentralization process.

For the longer term, the California state auditor's report bases its recommendations on a comprehensive vision statement that incorporates accountability measures for LACCD as well as the colleges. Spending controls need to be developed and implemented, and accountability needs to be enforced at all levels of operations.

The new governor of California, Gray Davis, has repeatedly proclaimed that education is his first priority. His primary focus is on public school K–12 reforms and the University of California. Although he did not mention California's community colleges and the California State Universities by name, these institutions play a pivotal role in educating California's population. The LACCD leadership should bring people together to design educational opportunities for the disadvantaged, those who are part of net outflow from LACCD, the limited English proficient, and those seeking naturalization to become citizens.

The colleges need to find ways to make themselves competitive in many arenas, including the search for external funding and economic development opportunities. They also need to learn to institutionalize economic development activities through their curriculum and staffing activities. Conflicting values theory attempts to reconcile the disparate educational functions with the needs of a society and an economy. This is an appropriate guide for the community colleges, which have a variety of constituents and missions. If the leadership of LACCD can maintain a broad perspective on its many functions and be inclusive in its planning, institutional change can occur that maximizes outcomes by focusing on the strengths in the LACCD and its nine-college system.

References

AFT Faculty Guild, Local 1521. *LACCD 2000: Increasing Institutional Effectiveness and Accountability Through Educational and Budgetary Decentralization.* Los Angeles: AFT Faculty Guild, May 19, 1998.

California Citizens Commission on Higher Education. *A State of Learning: California Higher Education in the Twenty-First Century. A Report from the California Citizens Commission on Higher Education.* Los Angeles: California Citizens Commission on Higher Education, 1998.

California Community Colleges, Board of Governors. *California Community Colleges, 2005: A Strategic Response for Enabling Community Colleges to Make a Defining Difference in the Social and Economic Success of California in the Twenty-First Century.* Sacramento: California Community Colleges, Board of Governers, 1998.

California State Auditor, Bureau of State Audits. *Los Angeles Community College District: Proposed Reforms Have Not Fully Addressed Past Problems and Create a New Set of Challenges.* Report no. 97107. Sacramento: California State Auditor, Bureau of State Audits, Dec. 1998.

Erickson, L. J. *The Los Angeles Community College District Crisis, 1981–1987.* Los Angeles: Los Angeles Valley College, 1997.

Fujimoto, J. "Educational Implications for Mainstreaming New Americans." Paper presented at the National Conference of the American Association of Higher Education, Chicago, Illinois, April 1992. (ED 343652)

Fujimoto, J. *Fulfilling the Promise: From Amnesty to Citizenship. Part I: The Los Angeles Mission College Experience.* Los Angeles: California Community College Educators for New Californians, 1994. (ED 375866)

Office of Instruction and Student Services. *Information Digest, The Los Angeles Community Colleges.* [http://www.laccd.edu/edsvcs/iriu.htm]. August 1999.

Office of Research and Planning. *Los Angeles Community College District, Los Angeles Community Colleges Student Characteristics, Fall 1997.* Los Angeles: Los Angeles Community College District, 1998.

Yoneji, N. "Response to March 10, 1996 L.A. Times Editorial, Valley Section." *Los Angeles Times,* Mar. 26, 1996.

JACK FUJIMOTO, *a former campus president and vice chancellor in the California Community College system, is a consultant to the chancellor.*

6

The dynamic tension created by Phoenix residents' rising
social demands and the reality of scarce resources presents
the Maricopa system with a major challenge.

Profiles in Urban Challenges: Confronting Maricopa's Social and Economic Agenda

Paul A. Elsner

Arizona's Maricopa Community Colleges are faced with a myriad of urban challenges. Four of the campuses are in the city of Phoenix, an urban center experiencing rapidly changing demographics, growth, and social dislocations.

The fundamental challenge to Maricopa planners is how to carry out a necessary urban-based social agenda in view of scarce resources, the unenthusiastic support of state-level policy shapers, and Maricopa's own internal disagreement about mission and purpose. On top of the rising social demands placed on the Maricopa system rests a pro-growth, free-market energy that puts Maricopa in the middle of the economic development initiatives of its region.

All of these forces create a dynamic tension in the Maricopa Community College system, yet these forces and tensions are not necessarily well sorted out in the national community. They certainly are strongly felt at the regional and local levels. Such is the typical plight of many urban community colleges.

The Maricopa System

The Maricopa Community Colleges form part of a statewide system of locally organized college districts. All but five counties in the state have organized community college districts. The Maricopa County Community College District—its official name—is referred to as the Maricopa Community Colleges (MCCD).

MCCD is one of the largest, if not the largest, community college districts in the nation. In all, it serves more than 240,000 persons year round. MCCD consists of ten colleges and several centers, with a combined enrollment of approximately 190,000 credit students. Enrollment in noncredit and special interest courses reaches close to 50,000. Four of Maricopa's ten colleges are in Phoenix, and three of those are in the inner city. Urban community colleges face the greatest challenges of poverty and social complexity. Their demographics call for greater attention to diversity and student preparedness.

There are many hallmarks for which the Maricopa Community Colleges are well known. Among these, its robust university transfer program stands out. Arizona State University (ASU), a large, comprehensive, research university in Tempe, claims that upwards of 65 percent of their upper-division students consists of transfers from the Maricopa Community Colleges. The University of Phoenix alone reports that 80 percent of its graduates have completed a major portion of their lower-division course work at one of the Maricopa Community Colleges. MCCD's assessment data indicate that Maricopa's students do as well as or better than university freshmen as they progress to the upper divisions (Day, 1999).

Another hallmark is Maricopa's strong presence in industry and corporate training, a strength that grows out of a concerted effort on Maricopa's part to network with the economic development apparatus in Arizona and the Maricopa County region. On any given day, the Maricopa Community Colleges will have fifty to sixty industries under contract in training arrangements. This group of industries alone accounts for a major share of Arizona's high annual job creation rate of 85,000 to 100,000 new jobs (Jarman, 1999). Much of this incredible growth is due to Maricopa's extraordinary ability to bid successfully for and compete with other training providers, both private and public. Maricopa's training capacity is the central attraction for the many new industries that relocate to Maricopa County.

The Maricopa Community Colleges' training capacity has become part of the economic portfolio for this state. This portfolio goes out all over the world because the Phoenix area recruits industries worldwide. The competition extends beyond Austin, Sacramento, and Salt Lake City. Economic development professionals now must compete for their new industries with Singapore, suburban Brussels, Ireland, and hundreds of other favorable business environments.

The Maricopa Community Colleges' corporate training is linked with other influential business climate factors, such as an advantageous taxation policy, an unfettered regulatory environment, and Arizona's favorable quality of life. While many economic development clusters have been established in Arizona's strategic efforts to attract industry, high technology has been one of the dominant training areas to which Maricopa has responded.

Among the sixty-seven companies currently contracting with the Maricopa Community Colleges are Orbital Sciences, Inc., Jerrik Connection Devices, Matson Navigating Company, Air Products and Chemicals, Inc., Motorola, and Intel. The Maricopa Community Colleges trained over 85,000 person-hours in 1998 for Motorola alone—the equivalent of the entire enrollment of Phoenix College or Scottsdale Community College, both very large campuses.

The Maricopa Community Colleges serve many other occupational clusters. They are the largest providers of health services training in Arizona. Over four thousand courses are activated each year from Maricopa course banks. Those courses cover over four hundred occupational or career clusters.

Rio Salado College, also a Maricopa Community College, is a nontraditional, distance-education college offering 128 Internet courses. It provides every form of distance education and has enjoyed an annual enrollment growth of between 12 and 15 percent over the past five years.

These hallmarks do not include Maricopa's massive technology infrastructure, its collaboration with schools, its service-learning agenda, or its role in training a national cadre of leaders. Maricopa's Chair Academy targets twenty-two thousand division chairs and academic leaders in the United States, United Kingdom, Australia, Canada, and the Netherlands, and it plans to expand its initiatives into southeast Asia. The academy has a history of answering some of the urban problems and issues that face multicollege institutions in such areas as technology transformation, conflict resolution, and multicultural programs.

Another leadership initiative developed by the Maricopa Community Colleges and funded by the Ford Foundation is the National Institute for Leadership Development (NILD). Carrole Wolin, NILD president, reports that approximately four thousand women have completed the NILD program and have moved on to all levels of management and leadership. Wolin also reports that 80 percent of women currently sitting in chief executive officer positions in higher education around the country are products of the NILD. Among the many urban chancellors or presidents are Jerry Sue Thornton, chancellor of the Cuyahoga Community College District in Cleveland; Beverly Simone, president of Madison Area Technical College; and Tessa Martinez Pollack, president of Glendale Community College in Arizona.

The Maricopa Community Colleges were charter members of Campus Compact, a consortium set up at Brown and Georgetown universities to promote service-learning in university and college settings. The MCCD operates the National Center for Campus Compact for Community Colleges. Students at the Maricopa Community Colleges are networked with hundreds of community-based organizations (CBOs) for volunteer and service-learning experiences. In no small way, Maricopa is involved with constructing and carrying out important social agendas that affect the quality of urban life in this area. Some of the activities range from working with youth vulnerable to becoming gang members, to working with the homeless and Habitat for Humanity. The colleges celebrate an "Into the Streets" movement each year during which students fan out into the cities with hundreds of community-based service-learning projects.

Meeting Urban Challenges

The Maricopa Community Colleges shape urban policy in a significant way. In 1990, MCCD developed the charter for the only coalition in the nation of large urban community college districts. R.C. 2000, an organization that promotes renewal and change (R.C.) for the future, now has twenty-five members, including most of the chancellors and presidents of the largest community colleges in the country.

R.C. 2000's executive director, Janet Beauchamp, is housed at Maricopa and also serves in this capacity for the Phoenix Think Tank, a collaboration of the Maricopa Community Colleges and several high schools, elementary school districts, businesses, and CBOs in Phoenix's inner city. Think Tank members, like their R.C. 2000 counterparts, represent a striking demographic profile of urban community colleges. They include eight high schools in the Phoenix Union High School District, which have approximately 60 percent minority enrollments. The several inner-city elementary school districts are mostly Hispanic in enrollment, sometimes as high as 85 to 100 percent.

R.C. 2000 publishes *The Urban Report,* which discusses local urban development issues. Articles include programs about outreach, poverty, neighborhood rebuilding, housing, arts organizations, and other community-based organizations and initiatives. Meetings are held twice every year in a different member city and focus on an urban topic. At the Community College of Denver, the U.S. secretary of housing briefed members on housing issues in the city. When the group met in Atlanta, the topic of race was on the agenda, and members heard from speakers such as Maynard Jackson, former mayor of Atlanta, and a locally elected congressman whose agendas have included urban issues.

The Maricopa Community Colleges, like many other urban community college districts, are faced with balancing several large forces, two of which stand out for having placed enormous pressure on urban community colleges. The first is the current popular bias that open, free-market forces determine our best destiny. The second major force is that technology is redefining our roles, if not eclipsing us. We are faced with the responsibility of maintaining some kind of viable internal and academic community in the face of these two large forces. We cannot begin to achieve a stable academic community without addressing the effects of these enormous forces—the market and technology—as well as rapidly changing demographics.

Woven into these forces is the perplexing question of how much urban community colleges should be engaged in the social agenda. Very high levels of poverty are disproportionately present in cities. Although there is rural poverty, the incidence of violent crime, gang-related activities, and drug addiction does not plague rural areas with the intensity that a typical urban neighborhood must confront.

In addition, community colleges in urban cities live in the local cauldron of electoral politics: special interest groups, manpower commissions, and CBOs that are fiercely competitive about prerogative and territory. Community colleges are increasingly accountable to the mandates of their own boards, the mayor's agenda, the CBOs in their areas, churches and charitable groups, and youth and poverty organizations. Urban community colleges are likened to a suspended force field with special interests, pulled this way and that, depending on the power valences of principal players in the community.

The Demographic Challenge. Community colleges as a whole are a remarkable educational segment. Of the more than 14 million students enrolled in higher education, community colleges enroll in excess of 7 million. An estimated 48 percent of African Americans, 58 percent of Hispanics, and 50 percent of Native Americans in higher education are enrolled in community colleges (Wilds and Wilson, 1998). To complicate demographics further, the Maricopa system enrolls the largest number of F-1 (foreign visa) students in the country.

The Challenge of the Social Agenda. Community colleges understand and accept their role in social responsibility by not turning their backs on their constituent groups who are struggling to make it out of dislocation, separation, or poverty. Policymakers at the state level, however, do not appear to be concerned with the social agenda. If anything, policy shapers try to pare back urban community college functions to central core purposes and general education fundamentals like reading, writing, and math, largely because of the pressures from employers who complain about the low educational achievements of their employees.

The Maricopa Community Colleges have heeded these admonitions. However, less than 8 percent of the annual budget of $614 million comes from the state of Arizona. Thus, the Maricopa Community Colleges have enjoyed a greater sense of self-determination than most other community colleges in the United States because they have broken away from total dependency on the state and have broadened the revenue structure to include significant amounts of restricted funds, grants, and self-generating government and corporate contracts. These restricted funds alone account for over $100 million of the Maricopa budget. Still, the Maricopa Community Colleges are not largely a locally supported system because only 57 percent of the budget comes from a local ad valorem tax. Therefore, a great number of socially purposeful agendas have had to be funded out of the already limited resources.

The Maricopa Community Colleges operate an alternative high school near Chandler-Gilbert Community College, a charter high school at GateWay Community College, and several concurrent enrollment programs with about four thousand students taking courses at the community colleges while simultaneously taking courses in high school. Maricopa also supports a youth center, Espiritu; programs that work with troubled youth like Project Challenge (a basic training boot camp for students at a nearby former military base); and the Genesis Program, which has pulled students out of gangs and put them into achievement-oriented programs.

The Maricopa colleges are in the process of proposing a strong math and science high school as a charter school to one of the inner-city elementary school districts. Many of the superintendents of Phoenix's inner-city schools complain that when their students go on to high school, they are lost and often drop out in their freshman or sophomore years. Hence there is a motivation for the inner-city elementary school districts in Phoenix to create their own charter schools or their own high schools.

There is much philosophical and role conflict in this for MCCD. For example, how much erosion of the public school system is occurring because of the promotion of voucher systems and charter schools by the conservative policy shapers in the state? Another conflict centers around mission. Even the Maricopa Community Colleges have board members who are willing to debate the philosophical premises that take the colleges away from their original mission of being a two-year, postsecondary-only community college system with more traditional junior college transfer functionality. This is a debate Maricopa expects to see escalate and to go on for years to come. It will depend on future leadership to resolve these issues.

Maricopa always has struggled with the social agenda, and it has done so in spite of mission charges and differences of opinion among its internal community. As chancellor of the Maricopa Community Colleges for more than twenty-two years, I often had to forge ahead with Maricopa's social agenda even in the face of vocal opposition, on the assumption that if one does not move forward, the social agenda will not be carried out.

Market Forces Challenging the Urban Mission. One of the issues that urban community colleges like Maricopa must face is how much of its mission should be shaped to adapt to the demographic realities of our community. Up to this point Maricopa has done quite well and one way or another has found the resources to work in collaboration with community agencies and other funding structures to get the job done.

One of the most promising structures has been the Maricopa/Phoenix Think Tank, a dynamic collaboration of inner-city interests including elementary schools, high schools, corporations, CBOs, and the Maricopa Community College District as convener and staff support for its operations and programs. The three main program thrusts comprise an effective urban agenda for community colleges. Simply conceived and carried out, the Think Tank has strategically designed and achieved the following goals:

- The ExCEL project has integrated and coordinated staff as well as organizational development among nine elementary school districts, eight high schools, the Maricopa Community College District, Arizona State University, CBOs, and the business community. The project already has strengthened technology transfer and training of school personnel. It has aligned science and math objectives under a National Science Foundation Systemic Initiative grant, and it has created a strategic community of several staff development coordinators and directors for all Think Tank member organizations. Maybe even more important, math scores in the elementary schools in Phoenix's inner-city have risen to surpass statewide averages because of the ExCEL program.
- The Connectivity Project has stressed a seamless transition from segment to segment by facilitating concurrent high school–community college enrollments at Maricopa. More than four thousand high school students, largely

from the inner-city high schools, participate. In addition, 65 percent of ASU's upper-division classes are former Maricopa Community College students. In its early days the Think Tank promoted the concept that students in all segments of education, from kindergarten through graduate school, belong to all of us. We have a responsibility for every child in urban elementary, middle, and high school.

• Family Resource Centers work with inner-city schools whose students are besieged by family poverty, separation and loss, dislocation and constant uprooting, and daily violence and extreme danger. If a child appears in school with signs of physical abuse, it can take a teacher or a counselor all day to obtain a human resources or child protective services referral. Moreover, instant judgment is required to manage the situation.

Family Resource Centers, staffed by seasoned human services personnel, take a tremendous burden off the shoulders of the schools. Moreover, they have become trusted resources for parents, children, teachers, and community agencies.

After a professionally and time-tested model of the Family Resource Centers worked in the Murphy Elementary School District, nine other centers were established at elementary school sites, all serving similar inner-city locations. The leadership given to this expansion came from several collaborators, but a creative Honeywell executive and a member of the Phoenix chapter of the Alliance for Business provided the early leadership for this project.

These projects rely on organizations like the Boys and Girls Clubs, CBOs, local churches, and state and local welfare and assistance personnel like Arizona's Department of Economic Security.

The Technology Challenge. Technology provides a barrier to thousands of students, maybe millions, who have neither the cultural advantage nor the personal wealth to participate in the new economies. The basic issue for urban community colleges is that technology is inequitably distributed in the population. To cite a recent event, a school in one of Arizona's poorest areas had its only computer stolen. In contrast, in a nearby suburban school, students have their own computers and even their own web pages.

The Maricopa Community Colleges have insisted that as an urban district, it will always support public open-entry, open-exit labs with thousands of personal computers accessible to the public. One such center at Glendale Community College has 420 work stations in its High Tech Center. Another Maricopa college will have 1,500 public work stations in its Information Commons, a public access center for all students regardless of their background.

The Maricopa Think Tank has received grants to train all of the teachers in its inner-city member elementary schools and high schools on the applications of the Internet. About three thousand teachers, through a League for Innovation grant with the Stevens Institute of Technology, will receive full training on the use of the Internet and the design of web-based services for students.

Conclusion

The Maricopa Community Colleges have launched many socially important agendas that serve urban communities. There is still much to do, and an abundance of challenges and obstacles must be overcome. However, the forces of the free market, demographics, and technology are embedded in the stories to come of the future.

References

Day, M. *Report on the Board ENDS.* Phoenix: Office of Institutional Research, Mar. 1999.
Jarman, M. "Phoenix Area Jobs to Double in Twenty-Five Years." *Arizona Republic Newspaper,* Mar. 30, 1999.
Wilds, D. J., and Wilson, R. *Minorities in Higher Education: 1997–98.* Washington, D.C.: American Council on Education, 1998.

PAUL A. ELSNER retired as chancellor of the Maricopa Community College system in June 1999.

7

Community colleges on the periphery of the nation's cities increasingly are acquiring urban characteristics and experiencing urban challenges that require innovative solutions.

Baltimore County: A College and Community in Transition

Irving Pressley McPhail, Ronald C. Heacock

The Community College of Baltimore County (CCBC) is a new, multicampus, comprehensive community college offering a wide array of career, transfer, and continuing-education programs. Formed in 1998, CCBC was created from a merger of three established and separate colleges in Baltimore County: Catonsville Community College, Dundalk Community College, and Essex Community College. The new CCBC is the product of the political, economic, and social forces of its external environment; the culture and history of its internal environment; and the integration of demands from external and internal constituencies. Its creation has been tumultuous, lengthy, and costly. Yet despite its difficult birth, CCBC can and should be the agent that shapes its own future, the future of its students, and the future of Baltimore County.

As the service area of the college is quickly becoming an urban as opposed to a suburban landscape, the college has an opportunity to prepare for the challenges that urban community colleges face and can serve as an example to other colleges in a similar state of transition. The challenge of a new urban community college is to educate a population that is on average poorer, less prepared, increasingly minority, and increasingly first-generation college. These characteristics describe a group that is vulnerable and difficult to bring into the economic mainstream. They are also more likely to need greater support than did the county's once-traditional suburban students. In addition, the resources to accomplish these challenges are usually more limited. CCBC is facing the problem of doing more with less.

For the college to assume the lead role in the drama of institutional renewal rather than merely serving as the stage, it must have a vision or set of guiding principles. This vision serves as a compass and helps the college make reasonable and consistent choices among alternative routes as it navigates the future. The vision must be grounded in the challenges that confront colleges in the information age. It must speak to the changes in the community at large, serve students, and unite the college community in a time of internal transition.

This vision can be found in the principles of the learning college as set forth by Barr (1998), Barr and Tagg (1995), and O'Banion (1997a, 1997b). These principles give direction for strategic planning, which for CCBC are contained in *Learning First,* the CCBC strategic plan. If actions, operational planning, resource allocation, and budgetary commitment support the strategic plan, the college's capacity for future change should be strengthened. To understand the role of the college and the importance of its vision and planning for the future, we must first look at the social, political, and economic factors that comprise its environment.

Baltimore County: A New Urban Landscape

Baltimore County is in transition. Once a rapidly growing and thriving suburban county, it is now classified by the Maryland Office of Planning as an older, suburban, and increasingly urban county. Today the county tends to have more in common with cities than it does with its rural and suburban past. Urban woes, such as underemployment, unemployment, violence, substance abuse, homelessness, crime, single-parent families, and poverty, are increasing in the county.

From the end of World War II until the 1970s, the county saw rapid growth and continuing prosperity relative to normal economic cycles. As a result, the county is largely composed of first-generation suburbs, populated in the 1950s and 1960s by working- and middle-class residents moving from Baltimore City. Baltimore City, which is surrounded by Baltimore County and is a separate political entity, has declined, as have many older urban areas. From 1990 to 1997, Baltimore City lost 78,800 residents, mainly to Baltimore County. Once largely young, white, and upwardly mobile, the county now sees an influx of poorer and minority families migrating out from a declining urban city.

Baltimore County is, in turn, surrounded by the newer, suburban counties. During the 1980s thousands of Baltimore County residents left for the newer, suburban jurisdictions of Carroll, Howard, Harford, and Frederick counties. Many of these migrating residents were from the middle and upper-middle classes. The older suburbs, in close proximity to Beltway interchanges, welcomed the newer, and generally poorer, residents who left Baltimore City for Baltimore County. During the 1980s and 1990s, Baltimore County's growth rate was a modest 3.7 percent, similar to that of an older suburb. The new suburban counties, by contrast, grew at a much greater rate. Howard County had a growth rate of 57 percent during the 1980s, and Carroll had a 28 percent increase. This differential continued in the 1990s, with Howard, Harford, and Carroll growing at 19.8 percent, 16.4 percent, and 14.8 percent, respectively.

Baltimore County's population is aging and growing poorer. In 1995, its median income was the lowest of any other county in the region. Between

1990 and 1993, the county's poverty rate increased from 5.5 percent to 8 percent as it drew poor city residents.

A recent study commissioned by the Citizens Planning and Housing Association (Orfield, 1997) concluded that as the population continues to migrate into older suburban areas, crime, poverty, and subpar schools will follow. It found that pockets of Baltimore County are beginning to evidence the decay traditionally associated with cities. Myron Orfield (1997), an authority on the dynamics of metropolitan areas, stated that "poverty and social and economic need have concentrated and are deepening in central-city neighborhoods and older suburban places. This concentration destabilizes schools and neighborhoods, is associated with increases in crime and results in the flight of middle-class families and businesses" (p. 6). This neglect is evident in Baltimore County in areas such as Essex, Dundalk, Catonsville, Middle River, and Garrison. Orfield maintains that Baltimore County will grow poorer every year.

In addition, the county and metropolitan area has experienced a loss of traditional manufacturing. Bethlehem Steel, once the foundation of the eastern Baltimore economy, has declined precipitously since the 1970s. Projected job growth has followed the population growth to the suburbs as well. Between 1990 and 1996, job losses occurred in almost every part of Baltimore City and in the inner suburbs of Baltimore County, while the biggest growth in job opportunities occurred in Harford, Howard, and Carroll counties.

As with many other regions, Baltimore is seeking to create jobs and industries that are attuned to the global and increasingly technological economy. Economic development and the revitalization of older neighborhoods are important to the county as it seeks to meet the challenges of the postindustrial economy that brought so much prosperity to the region.

The Political Arena

CCBC is a quasi-governmental agency, overseen directly by a governor-appointed board of trustees. There are fifteen trustees on the board: two from each of the seven Baltimore County Council Districts and one from the county at large. Although not specified in the enabling legislation, trustees are normally appointed based on the recommendation of local political officials. All community colleges in Maryland are county based and receive funding from both the county and the state, as well as from student tuition and fees. The Maryland Higher Education Commission (MHEC), the state higher education authority, enforces regulations established for all community colleges, monitors and approves academic programs, and reviews state-mandated finance and accountability reports. Still, for the most part, the governance is remote. The state regulates through legislation and regulations that establish parameters for their oversight. Although the state also funds the community colleges, this funding is based on a formula, and there is no negotiation over amounts. Normally the relationship and governance issues related to the state cover the community colleges as a group and not single institutions.

County governments in the state can exert differing levels of control. Most county governments exert little control over their community colleges, allowing the board of trustees to exert control and oversight. Budgetary controls are normally limited to negotiations concerning the percentage change in the overall budget with the occasional specifications for large projects or programs. However, in the case of Baltimore County the level of control has been extensive in recent years, resulting in the creation of CCBC. The primary means by which this control has been exercised is through the budget process. The level of oversight and analysis has gone all the way down to the cost center and individual project level.

The Community College of Baltimore County: The Recent Past

The conditions that changed the county have shaped the community college. During the late 1970s and early 1980s, the county was wealthy enough to fund three independent community colleges, the only county in the state of Maryland to do so. However, as difficult fiscal realities forced the county to tighten its belt, it looked to the colleges to supply part of those savings. Funding for the colleges remained flat for a number of years, and the colleges found it increasingly difficult to operate. As budgets grew tighter, the colleges developed strategies to maintain control of their operations. For example, they kept funds off budget, used an increasing number of part-time faculty to teach, and used vacant positions to fund other functions. The loss of dollars made the colleges seek increasing flexibility to cope with the day-to-day vagaries of the management of a complex organization. This strategy, while well intentioned, led to a loss of credibility and increased animosity with the county and the county budget office.

In 1995, legislation was introduced to combine the three colleges into one. The initial legislation created the Community Colleges of Baltimore County, a merger of the three colleges under a single small system office. Savings were to be achieved by combining the institutional support functions of the three colleges. The management model employed to govern this new college was matrix management, a system that gave each of the college presidents and many college employees systemwide responsibilities.

Clashes over the level of savings to be achieved, the disposition of those funds, and other perceived economies led to increasing animosity among the board of trustees, the county government, and the chancellor of the system. Further, employees of the colleges, especially the faculty, became increasingly disenchanted with the merger of the colleges. These conditions and the environment of distrust that had developed over the years resulted in increasing conflict, culminating in an unprecedented $2.3 million reduction in county appropriations for the college in fiscal year 1997; six months later, the first chancellor was terminated. An interim chancellor was appointed, the board of trustees was restructured, and a new board chair was brought in. Finally, new legislation was introduced to complete the merger of the three colleges into a single college with three campuses. Today the chancellor of CCBC reports directly to the board, and the three campus presidents report directly to the chancellor. The system office has been increased in size with the creation of new vice chancellor positions, and matrix management has been all but eliminated.

Approximately twenty thousand credit students per semester and more than thirty thousand continuing-education students are enrolled at CCBC each year. Although still the largest college in the state of Maryland, the college has experienced enrollment declines from its peak of twenty-five thousand credit students per semester in 1991. Reasons for the decline include shifting county demographics, an aging population, and the turmoil caused by the merger of the colleges. The student characteristics reflect the transition to a more urban environment. An increasing percentage is minority students, now approximately a third of all students. More students are immigrants, and the number for whom English is a second language grows daily. Almost 10 percent of CCBC's students come from Baltimore City, even though the tuition rates are much higher for noncounty residents. CCBC's students are poorer in both resources and preparation. Ever increasing numbers require remedial education and additional services. More and more are first-generation college students. Clearly the traditional way of doing business and providing services will not meet the demands of this new, neglected majority.

CCBC, like all other social institutions, exists within the realm of a larger social, political, and economic environment. However, although the environment affects the college, the college can also affect its environment. CCBC is part of a complex, dynamic, open system. The question is not whether change will occur, but who will control the change: the college or its external environment. If the college allows the external environment to serve as the principal change agent, then it operates by merely reacting to environmental forces. If the college assumes control in the recasting, it can function proactively and in accordance with its mission and strategic priorities.

Learning First: A Vision for the College and the Community

The foundation that must guide both CCBC's internal commitment and its ability to adapt to the external environment is a vision or set of guiding principles that give meaning to the institution's actions. Only when an institution is centered and has a vision can it adjust to the internal conflicts that are brought about by change and to the external pressures that will stand in its way. Without such a vision, an organization will quickly lose sight of its purpose and confuse it with the day-to-day management of the forces that seek to change and influence it. In other words, actions will become purpose when no purpose previously existed.

The challenge that a new leader faces in a time of turmoil is to provide a vision and direction for the institution. A leader cannot command or control the community and conditions that surround his institution. Indeed, a leader cannot even control his own organization, if *control* means a mechanistic direction of one's will throughout the organization. The formal authority a leader has is limited—more limited than most realize. A leader must lead; that is, she must be able to persuade those who work for her that her vision is worthwhile and should be followed. A leader must also use this vision in dealing with leaders and groups in the external environment with whom mutual relationships exist. The heart of the informal authority that a leader needs can be grounded in a vision that addresses the needs of those in both internal and external environments.

Clearly the changes facing the college and its students are one and the same. The direction established by the chancellor was that of creating a student-centered learning environment for the colleges. This plan was set forth in the college's strategic plan, *Learning First,* which incorporates the principles of the learning college into a series of strategic directions that will make CCBC a premier learning-centered, single-college, multicampus institution in an increasingly urban environment. A learning college (1) creates substantive change in individual learners; (2) engages learners in the learning process as full partners, assuming primary responsibility for their own choices; (3) creates and offers as many options for learning as possible; (4) assists learners to form and participate in collaborative learning activities; (5) defines the roles of learning facilitators by the needs of the learners; and (6) succeeds only when improved and expanded learning can be documented for its learners (O'Banion, 1997a). The learning college provides an appropriate environment and direction for the college in a number of ways.

With these six principles as the foundation, a strategic plan was created to promote the development of CCBC into a learning college in the context of its changing urban environment. *Learning First* contains seven strategic directions: one core and six supporting strategic directions. The core strategic direction is Student Learning. The six supporting directions are Learning Support, Learning College, Infusing Technology, Management Excellence, Embracing Diversity, and Building Community.

- Student Learning sets learning as CCBC's core value and direction, and the system judges all other outcomes based on this proposition. CCBC's goal is to provide a high-quality learning-centered education that maximizes student learning and makes students partners in their education. Students should be able to frame and achieve their educational goals and develop skills for the twenty-first century.
- Learning Support provides for a comprehensive and responsive support system that increases access and recognizes the student as central to the learning process. The goals here are to increase student retention and success, create seamless instructional and student support services, improve student skills assessment and course placement, and increase access to programs and services for the community at large.

- The Learning College provides direction for the transformation of CCBC into a learning college, promoting free exchange of ideas, innovation, continuous improvement through organizational learning, and assessment through a comprehensive institutional effectiveness and evaluation system.
- Infusing Technology recognizes and promotes the use of new instructional technologies to strengthen student learning and the use of technology to improve the effectiveness and efficiency of college operations. The college is also committed to serving the county and becoming the primary provider of technology workforce training programs in Baltimore County.
- Management Excellence is designed to further the efficient and effective use of resources by linking planning and budgeting. In addition, it promotes low-cost access to the college.
- Embracing Diversity focuses on attracting and retaining a diverse faculty, staff, and student community; advancing a learning environment that embraces and values diversity; and incorporating diversity into the curriculum and recognizing diverse learning styles.
- Building Community advances CCBC as an active member of its larger community, taking a leading role in workforce training, and forming partnerships to support economic and community development efforts. Community advances CCBC as an active member of its larger community, taking a leading role in workforce training, and forming partnerships to support economic and community development efforts.

New Directions. How will this plan and its strategic directions address the problems of CCBC's transition to an urban community college and help the institution deal with its new student population? How will it help the system heal itself and become a new institution? How will it help CCBC become accountable in the eyes of its external environment? In developing the system's vision and strategic plan, these questions were at the center of discussions.

First, the plan recognizes that all learners deserve high-quality instruction appropriately linked to their experiences and backgrounds. This is extremely important for the growing number of minority students with diverse backgrounds and cultural learning styles. McPhail and McPhail (forthcoming) argue that the current theory base for the learning paradigm, which frames learning holistically, offers a powerful alternative to the atomistic model of the instruction paradigm. However, they conclude that a new theory more directly linking culture, information processing, and instruction is needed to transform classroom practice for culturally diverse learners. They propose a theory of cultural mediation in instruction as an extension of the conceptual base undergirding the learning paradigm. Such a theory offers the promise of student success for African American learners in the community college.

Second, it recognizes the need for access to learning "anyway, anyplace, anytime" (O'Banion, 1997a, p. 15). As the urban community increases the diversity of students and the number of nontraditional students, it must be prepared to meet their educational demands through a variety of learning programs. Such institutions must find ways of reaching out to urban learners. Distance learning and on-line learning must be widely available in order to provide convenient services to those who desperately need them while introducing them to the technology revolution.

Third, urban students need to be put at the center of the learning process. Persistence or a commitment to learning is the necessary condition for academic success. Many better students have been taught the value of education from childhood and have had strong role models. For many urban students, the role models are much less positive. By making students active partners in their learning, the college can involve them and teach them the skills necessary for future success. The college can instill the value of lifelong learning for lifelong success. This will empower students to become part of the mainstream of society.

Fourth, the learning college will bring technology into the lives of students. Numerous waves of change and improvement have bypassed the economically disadvantaged. The modern information economy presents a way to begin to include the have-nots and to introduce skills required for the information age. The critical shortage of information technology workers provides opportunities for urban community college students to begin their careers with high-paying jobs that do not require a baccalaureate degree. The system can begin to reach out to displaced and misplaced workers and provide them with a career path that will bring them into the mainstream of society. The technology learned will provide students the opportunity to enter the information technology workforce, introducing them to the digital age where nearly every aspect of our lives will be influenced by computers.

Toward a New Institution. The vision of a learning college promotes the idea of a learning community that engages all members of the college and provides them with a similar motivation and vision. Organizational goals are important, but they will not succeed unless the community of the institution believes and includes them in their daily actions. The learning college, as promoted by the chancellor and others in the institution, gives individuals a clear logic to focus on and a set of decision rules to use. Individuals can engage in a process that forces them to judge all their actions by the principles of the learning college.

As incorporated in the plan, the learning college recognizes continuous improvement and the development of a learning college. The acknowledgment of continuous learning and improvement is a powerful and important point in institutional renewal. An institution openly admits it is not perfect, and thus allows information and evaluation to be used as a tool for institutional renewal rather than a punitive instrument.

Accountability. Two strategic directions speak clearly to institutional relationships with the external community. Management excellence is CCBC's commitment to improve its fiscal relationship with the county government. If the college is to receive additional funding, then the local government must be convinced that the funds are being used wisely.

The strategic direction that speaks to building community also will serve to improve CCBC's relationship with its external environments. First, CCBC will be providing services the community needs, developing partnerships to improve workforce training and promote economic development. Second, the system will be recognized as a legitimate investment in the economic development of the community. The result will be to enhance CCBC's credibility with the county government that funds it. Engagement with local business will allow the college to create partnerships, internships, and employment possibilities for its students.

Finally, the emphasis of the learning college on evaluation should also help CCBC establish credibility with the local governing agency and with businesses in the local community.

A Look to the Future

Clearly there is much to be done. But most important, the doing requires direction and principles. In his work on management, Stephen Covey (1990) has expounded what he calls the notion of principle-centered living. Without principles at the center, most of what we do lacks meaning and coherence. We also have trouble distinguishing what is important and what we should do next. We act for the sake of acting. The notion of principle-centered living that Covey has propounded for human beings is no different from what has been proposed for Community College of Baltimore County.

References

Barr, R. B. "Obstacles to Implementing the Learning Paradigm: What It Takes to Overcome Them." *About Campus,* Sept.–Oct. 1998, pp. 18–25.

Barr, R. B., and Tagg, J. "From Teaching to Learning: A New Paradigm for Undergraduate Education." *Change,* 1995, 27 (6), 13–25.

Covey, S. *The Seven Habits of Highly Effective People.* New York: Simon & Schuster, 1990.

McPhail, I. P., and McPhail, C. J. "Transforming Classroom Practice for African-American Learners: Implications for the Learning Paradigm." In *Removing Vestiges: Research-Based Strategies to Promote Inclusion.* Forthcoming.

O'Banion, T. *Creating More Learning-Centered Community Colleges.* Mission Viejo, Calif.: League for Innovation in the Community College and People Soft, 1997a.

O'Banion, T. *A Learning College for the Twenty-First Century.* Phoenix: Oryx Press, 1997b.

Orfield, M. *Baltimore Metropolitics.* Baltimore, Md.: Citizen's Planning and Housing Association, Oct. 1997.

IRVING PRESSLEY MCPHAIL *is chancellor of the Community College of Baltimore County.*

RONALD C. HEACOCK *is vice chancellor for technology and planning at the Community College of Baltimore County.*

8

This annotated bibliography directs readers to additional publications that address topics pertinent to urban community colleges.

Sources and Information About Urban Community Colleges

Dana Scott Peterman, Carol A. Kozeracki

The following publications address four of the issues raised in this volume that are of particular importance to today's urban community colleges and their nontraditional, underprepared student body: workforce preparation, institutional assessment, English as a Second Language (ESL) and remedial education, and community partnerships. The previous chapters have examined individual institutions that have taken exemplary approaches to these topics and provided broader overviews of the issues that need to be considered. An underlying theme of many of these chapters is the importance of forming partnerships with the K–12 system, the business community, other colleges, and the local social service agencies to achieve desired goals.

Most ERIC documents (publications with ED numbers) can be viewed on microfiche at over nine hundred libraries worldwide. In addition, most may be ordered on microfiche or on paper from the ERIC Document Reproduction Service (EDRS) by calling (800) 443–ERIC. Journal articles are not available from EDRS, but they can be acquired through regular library channels or purchased from one of the following article reproduction services: Carl Uncover: [http://www.carl.org/uncover/], uncover@carl.org, (800) 787–7979; UMI: orders@infostore.com, (800) 248–0360; or IDI: tga@isinet.com, (800) 523–1850.

Workforce Preparation

These materials discuss the central role of community colleges in workforce development and preparation, and the need for the colleges to collaborate with employers and the community to ensure that the most appropriate types of training are being offered.

Fitzgerald, J., and Jenkins, D. *Making Connections: Community College Best Practices, in Connecting the Urban Poor to Education and Employment.* Chicago: University of Illinois, 1997. (ED 412 993)

Drawing on case studies of six urban community colleges, this report examines the community college mission with respect to economic and workforce development and describes model partnerships involving colleges, community-based organizations, government, and social service organizations to create pathways to employment for the urban poor. The report highlights the role of community colleges in the Annie E. Casey Jobs Initiative, designed to identify strategies for helping residents of inner-city neighborhoods to gain employment. It reviews the issues faced by the colleges in serving the urban poor, highlighting problems in linking noncredit and credit course systems. The following five characteristics of successful college programs also are described: strong commitment from college leadership, the provision of intensive support services, the formation of partnerships with social service and community organizations, innovative teaching methods, and active employer involvement. Finally, case studies are provided of successful efforts at the following colleges: El Paso Community College (Texas), LaGuardia Community College (New York), Miami-Dade Community College (Florida), Portland Community College (Oregon), San Diego Community College District (California), and Sinclair Community College (Ohio).

Building College and Community Services for Single Parents and Displaced Homemakers Project. Final Detailed Report. Austin, Tex.: Austin Community College, 1995. (ED 395 167)

The Building College and Community Services for Single Parents and Displaced Homemakers Project at Austin Community College (Texas) successfully achieved its goals for project year 1994–95. Formative and summative methods of evaluation show that the project developed cooperative linkages with more than twelve businesses and community organizations; actively recruited more than twelve hundred displaced homemakers and single parents, with more than 212 enrolling in vocational and technical education; effectively retained disadvantaged students through training and support services; and assisted in the school-to-work transition of graduating project participants. During the year, the project provided support services to 586 enrolled students who were single parents and displaced homemakers, with 90 of them receiving financial assistance to defray the cost of dependent care or textbooks and supplies. For the 82 students who received financial assistance from the project during fall and spring semesters, the average grade point average was 3.1, and 89 percent were retained through spring or summer. The project also provided assistance to 381 prospective single-parent students through career and educational planning or resource information. Students were highly satisfied with the services provided by the program. The program was also successful in helping students access alternative means of financial and other types of aid.

Adams, J. *Follow-Up Report on Employers of 1993–94 Graduates, Macomb Community College.* Warren, Mich.: Department of Research and Evaluation, 1995. (ED 386 226)

Each year, Macomb Community College (MCC) in Michigan conducts a study to determine the extent to which the training that the previous year's graduates received met the needs of area employers. Surveys were mailed to 305 employers in November 1994. The completed forms were received from 199 employers and responses were compared to findings from studies conducted over the previous four years. Study results include the following: (1) employers rated MCC's overall training at 4.33 on a 5-point scale, with employers consistently giving a rating of over 4.0 points in each of the past four years; (2) 83.0 percent of employers rated work opportunities as good or very good, while 82.0 percent rated the three-year outlook as good or very good; (3) 41.7 percent of the employers were from service industries; 25.6 percent were from manufacturing; 11.6 percent were from retail; 7.0 percent were from finance, insurance, and real estate; 2.5 percent were from transportation, communications, electric, gas, and sanitary services; 3.0 percent were from public administration; and 3.5 percent were unclassifiable; (4) on a 5-point scale, employers rated graduates' willingness to learn at 4.66, cooperation with coworkers at 4.62, cooperation with management at 4.58, personal initiative at 4.56, acceptance of responsibility at 4.53, attitude toward work at 4.51, and quality of work at 4.46; and (5) the lowest-rated areas of graduate characteristics were communication skills at 4.16 and technical knowledge and problem-solving skills at 4.11 each.

Gianini, P. C. "Economic Development: A Postmodern Dilemma." *Community College Journal,* 1997, 67 (6), 14–18.

This article discusses challenges facing community colleges that are related to economic development, changes in workforce needs, and changing student characteristics, such as the increasing numbers of adult students. The article describes efforts at Florida's Valencia Community College to address these challenges by becoming more learner centered. The author highlights efforts to link higher-order thinking skills to workforce training.

Institutional Effectiveness

The following works describe the efforts undertaken by a variety of urban community colleges to assess how effectively they are meeting the changing needs of their constituents.

Hudgins, J. L. "Using Indicators of Effectiveness to Demonstrate Accountability of Community Colleges." Paper presented at a meeting of the Texas Association of Community College Trustees and Administrators, Austin, Tex., Oct. 1995.

The institutional effectiveness movement has emerged on the higher education agenda because of increased global competition, decreased funding levels, and a loss of public confidence in higher education. Although the movement's emphasis on outcomes-based accountability has been integrated into state mandates, accreditation processes, and educational association agendas, colleges have been only minimally successful in integrating assessment into their organizational cultures. Efforts to tie assessment to funding have been generally unsuccessful. To achieve institutional effectiveness, institutions of higher education must focus on the following efforts: (1) developing more partnerships and using the collective resources of higher education; (2) improving communications with elected officials and policymakers; (3) involving faculty as partners in this process; and (4) addressing academic integrity and collective responsibility step by step. Since 1986, Midlands Technical College in South Carolina has been committed to the process of institutional effectiveness. It has developed a planning and management model that focuses on the evaluation of mission attainment, adopts critical success factors, identifies nineteen indicators of effectiveness, develops standards and benchmarks to measure progress, and uses a report card to keep trustees and the community informed of progress.

Institutional Effectiveness at Community and Technical Colleges in Texas: A State-Level Evaluation Process. Austin: Texas Higher Education Coordinating Board, 1995. (ED 388 358)

Based on recommendations from the state Task Force on Institutional Effectiveness, the Texas Higher Education Coordinating Board developed a new institutional review system designed to identify institutional and programmatic strengths and areas of concern, verify institutional outcomes and improvement efforts, identify exemplary programs and innovative ideas, and review progress toward college goals. Under the evaluation process, individual institutions are responsible for the deployment of financial, personnel, and physical plant resources. The process calls for yearly college self-studies to produce an annual data profile, and site visits to be conducted every four years by faculty, administrators, and board staff at state community and technical colleges. Evaluation is based on five critical success areas: (1) mission, or the institution's commitment to meeting the unique needs of the college's service area; (2) effective use of resources, assessing the commitment to policies and procedures to ensure quality planning and continuous improvement of programs; (3) access, focusing on the commitment to serving the diverse educational, social, and workforce development needs of the citizens of Texas; (4) achievement, reviewing the commitment to attaining the high-quality performance of students, programs, and services; and (5) quality, focusing on the commitment to meeting or exceeding standards of excellence in programs and services.

Myers, C. J., and Silvers, P. J. "Evaluating the College Mission Through Assessing Institutional Outcomes." Paper presented to the Association for Institutional Research Annual Forum, Chicago, May 1993. (ED 357 773)

To develop a new mission statement for Pima Community College (PCC) in Tucson, Arizona, a charrette process was used, in which detailed community input was solicited and incorporated as part of the mission statement development. Approximately one hundred representatives of the greater Tucson community, together with PCC staff, developed the mission statement for PCC in 1989. The same group convened several months later to develop a set of outcomes, or indicators of success (IS), directly linked to each of the twelve major areas of the college mission. After this second charrette, PCC's chancellor appointed an editorial committee of six representative charrette participants. In the ensuing months, the Institutional Effectiveness Committee, comprising administrators, faculty, and staff at PCC, prescribed one or more specific measures to assess each of the IS. The resulting specification table served as the basis for the collection, analysis, and reporting of assessment information. In May 1992, PCC's first annual report to the community was conducted, in which assessment results were presented to the original charrette groups. This process became a major support for program improvement at PCC and helped to meet new accreditation reporting requirements.

Wolverton, M. "Decision Making, Structure and Institutional Notions of Quality: A Case Study." Paper presented at the Annual American Educational Research Association Meeting, San Francisco, 1995. (ED 383 734)

Few studies have focused on the effects of systemic change and decentralized decision making on organizational structure and on an institution's notion of quality education. This study examined such interconnections at a multicampus metropolitan community college in an area of high crime, high unemployment, and racial tensions. More than 75 percent of the fifty-five thousand full-time students are people of color. Major reforms in the past two decades have established a core curriculum, a computerized advising and articulation system, and a student placement assessment system. A second set of reforms tied a comprehensive faculty development program, including continuing education and tuition reimbursement, to a faculty advancement system. Using the models of strategic planning, Total Quality Management, and systems thinking, the study traced the reform efforts over twenty years, demonstrating the cyclical spiraling of decision making at the college.

Oromaner, M., and Fujita, E. *Development of a Mission Statement for a Comprehensive Urban Community College.* Jersey City, N.J.: Hudson County Community College, 1993. (ED 363 363)

In 1977, a board of trustees was established for Hudson County Community College (HCCC), in New Jersey, with a mission to provide entry-level occupational certificates and associate of applied science degrees to students seeking preparation for employment. This original mission statement specifically stated that HCCC was not to be a comprehensive institution, but as the college's service area and the needs of its clientele changed, its mission statement was revised to adapt to the changing conditions. The first revision, undertaken in February 1983, widened the scope of the college's mission to include transfer-oriented curricula. In September 1992, representatives of the college and the external community initiated a six-month process to develop a new mission statement designed to reflect the addition of a liberal arts degree program. This process included reviews of exemplary mission statements, state documents, and educational and economic projections for Hudson County. In addition, questionnaires were sent to over 1,117 college and community members soliciting perceptions regarding an appropriate mission for HCCC. Responses were received from 367 individuals, representing HCCC students and faculty, Hudson County businesses, and community agencies. The resulting mission statement dedicates the college to general education, career education, developmental education, community services, professional development, transfer, and liberal arts. The 1993 mission statement is included in the publication.

ESL and Remedial Education

The following materials focus on two areas of the curriculum that are growing rapidly at urban community colleges: ESL and remediation.

McCabe, R. H., and Day, P. R. Jr. (eds.). *Developmental Education: A Twenty-First Century Social and Economic Imperative.* Laguna Hills, Calif.: League for Innovation in the Community College, 1998. (ED 421 176)

This monograph addresses the future of developmental education, identifying the major issues and providing examples of successful developmental programs. The first chapter, "Access and the New America of the Twenty-First Century," emphasizes several changes in American society that have affected access to education and developmental programs: the access revolution following World War II, technology, the aging of the population, immigration, poverty, family dynamics, employment, and enrollments in higher education. The second chapter, "Work, the Individual, and the Economy," discusses the changing nature of work and the resulting higher skills needed for employment, and welfare reform. Chapter Three, "What Works in Developmental Education," describes key components for developmental programs and provides several examples of successful programs. Chapter Four, "The Case for Developmental Education in the Twenty-First Century," offers several arguments that support the need for developmental programs. The remaining ten chapters contain data and descriptions of exemplary developmental education programs at community colleges throughout the country.

Littleton, R. Jr. *Developmental Education: Are Community Colleges the Solution?* Unpublished paper, 1998. (ED 414 982)

Although community colleges currently account for over half of minority enrollment in the United States, there is controversy regarding whether the colleges actually provide minority students with access to higher education or merely track them into low-level studies. Minority community college students face a number of barriers to success, such as inadequate college preparatory programs at inner-city high schools, inefficient or culturally biased assessment methods, and cuts in federal financial assistance. Moreover, nearly 90 percent of these students are in developmental programs, and many are adult learners, foreign born or educated, field-dependent learners with an external locus of control, or lacking self-esteem. Changes occurring in many states to remove developmental programs from universities also reduce the likelihood of minority students' achieving the bachelor's degree. To address these issues, colleges have begun to employ comprehensive and innovative methods to retain and matriculate minority students. New York's Borough of Manhattan Community College, for example, maintains a family day care network to train caregivers; operates a prefreshman immersion program for reading, math, and writing; and works with businesses to obtain alternative sources of financial aid. The author also examines the Minority Transfer Opportunities Program at Texas's Houston Community College and innovative articulation agreements developed by Ohio's Cuyahoga Community College.

Sainz, J., and Biggins, C. M. "Call for Excellence in Urban Education: The Community College's Answer." Paper presented at the Symposium on Developing Strategies for Excellence in Urban Education, Jersey City, N.J., 1993. (ED 364 264)

Although a college degree is an important economic and social resource, more and more students are entering colleges and universities without the basic skills necessary to achieve academic success, and a growing number are limited English speaking. Community colleges have an important role in ensuring vocational and academic success for these students, but it is important that they use creative and vigorous approaches instead of offering watered-down remedial curricula. Studies have consistently shown that approaches that provide basic skills training together with reasoning and critical thinking content are effective, and research and theories related to reading development suggest that the emphasis on mastering basic skills before advancing to higher-order ones is misguided. Furthermore, the importance of listening and speaking communication skills in any learning should not be overlooked, because they provide a way for low-literate students to bring their intellectual skills into the learning process. One program that gives students space for exploring and expanding ideas while developing their reading skills is Easy Steps to Reading Independence, which features a cumulative skill-building approach.

Kurzet, R. "Quality Versus Quantity in the Delivery of Developmental Programs for ESL Students." In J. M. Ignash (ed.), *Implementing Effective Policies for Remedial and Developmental Education.* New Directions for Community Colleges, no. 100. San Francisco: Jossey-Bass, 1997.

This chapter of a *New Directions for Community Colleges* volume devoted to remedial and developmental education discusses the recent influx of nonnative English speakers at Portland Community College. The issue of how to maintain the quantity of ESL education in the face of increasing demand is discussed. The author provides policy recommendations for effective and inclusive ESL instruction, including gaining a better understanding of who the students are, hiring only teachers who are appropriately trained, and increasing funding.

Ignash, J. "ESL Population and Program Patterns in Community Colleges." *ERIC Digest.* Los Angeles: ERIC Clearinghouse for Community Colleges, 1992. (ED 353 022)

Recent trends in immigration and foreign student enrollments are placing a growing demand on community colleges for ESL instruction. A 1991 study of course sections at 164 two-year colleges nationwide revealed that ESL had grown from 30 percent of all foreign language courses offered in 1983 to 51 percent in 1991. Also, the proportion of colleges offering ESL courses had grown from 26 percent in 1975 to 40 percent in 1991. ESL students tend to be concentrated in urban areas. They range from those unable to read and write in their native language to students with college degrees. Given the varied backgrounds of these students, community colleges often have developed ESL programs that respond to the specific needs of their local ESL population. Most commonly, ESL programs include instruction in listening comprehension, speaking, reading, writing, and grammar. Vocational ESL programs, which weave English-language skills into vocational subject areas, have been established at a number of two-year colleges.

Community Partnerships

These materials describe a broad variety of partnership efforts underway at community colleges that seek to support K–12 outreach and aid community development.

Merren, J., Hefty, D., and Soto, J. *School to College Linkages—New Models That Work.* Tucson, Ariz.: Pima County Community College District, 1997. (ED 413 967)

In an effort to link the K–12 systems with postsecondary education, Pima Community College (PCC) developed a number of outreach programs, one of which was the Summer Career Academy. During summer 1997, with the support of the Pima and Santa Cruz Counties School to Work Partnership and local business and industry, PCC conducted a series of twenty-one Summer Career Academies for high school juniors and seniors. The academies took place on PCC campuses and met for three weeks, combining a three-credit PCC course with field trips, guest speakers, and other supporting activities that provided students with career exploration opportunities. Fifteen occupational areas were offered, with the highest enrollment in computer science/Internet, health care, and emergency services. The School to Work grant covered the costs of the program. The academies were very successful, as indicated by the unexpectedly high enrollment of 403 students and a completion rate of nearly 91 percent. Students, who represented thirty-six high schools, including a number of alternative schools, stated that they enjoyed and benefited from the hands-on experience and numerous field trips. Suggestions for improvement included longer academies, better equipment, including computers, and more field trips and hands-on experience.

Donovan, R. A. *National Center for Urban Partnerships*. New York: National Center for Urban Partnerships, 1992. (ED 348 086)

An overview is provided of the development and activities of the National Center for Urban Partnerships, located on the Bronx Community College (BCC) campus in New York City. Introductory comments describe the center as a consortium of cities committed to improving student transfer through communitywide efforts. Cities must agree to meet four conditions when they join the consortium: designating an oversight leader; obtaining representation from top-level individuals in government, schools, colleges, business, and community-based organizations; developing strategic plans to help significant numbers of underserved urban students prepare for and obtain postsecondary degrees; and participating in data-gathering efforts. The bulk of this report consists of summaries of structure, accomplishments, and goals of each of the eleven participating city networks: the Bronx Education Alliance at BCC; the Denver Network at the Community College of Denver; the Houston Networks Team at Houston Community College; the Memphis Team at Memphis State University; the Miami-Dade Networks Team at Miami-Dade Community College; the Newark Team at Essex County College, New Jersey; the Northern Alameda County Regional Alliance for Educational Development at Peralta Community College District, Oakland, California; the Phoenix Think Tank at Maricopa County Community College District, Tempe, Arizona; the Santa Ana Networks Team at Rancho Santiago College, California; the Queens Urban Partnership at LaGuardia Community College, Long Island City, New York; and the Seattle Coalition for Educational Equity at Seattle Community College District.

McGrath, D. (ed.). *Creating and Benefiting from Institutional Collaboration: Models for Success*. New Directions for Community Colleges, no. 103. San Francisco: Jossey-Bass, 1998. (ED 423 015)

This volume highlights various long-term collaborative efforts among schools that were initiated by external funding. Several of the chapters describe efforts of the Ford Foundation's Urban Partnership Program. Articles include "Lessons from a Long-Term Collaboration" (Lindsay M. Wright and Rona Middleberg); "Creating Structural Change: Best Practices" (Janet E. Lieberman); "An Urban Intervention That Works: The Bronx Corridor of Success" (Michael C. Gillespie); "The Role of Rural Community Colleges in Expanding Access and Economic Development" (Hector Garza and Ronald D. Eller); "The Partnership Paradigm: Collaboration and the Community College" (Sara Lundquist and John S. Nixon); "The Collaborative Leader" (Carolyn Grubbs Williams); "Building Local Partnerships: Contributions of a National Center" (Barbara Schaier-Peleg and Richard A. Donovan); "Funding Collaboratives" (L. Steven

Zwerling); "No Pain, No Gain: The Learning Curve in Assessing Collaboratives" (Laura I. Rendón, Wendy L. Gans, and Mistalene D. Calleroz); and "Sources and Information: Community Colleges and Collaboration" (Erika Yamasaki). As the contributors to this volume emphasize, collaboration must be understood as both a distinctive process and a particular type of interorganizational structure.

Santiago, I. S. "Hostos Community College and the Bronx Center: A Model for a Community College Partnership in Urban Community Development." Paper presented at the American Association of Community Colleges Annual Convention, Washington, D.C., 1994. (ED 368 444)

In 1992, Hostos Community College (HCC), in the Bronx, New York, began participating in the Bronx Center project, a partnership among government, community organizations, and private groups to develop a comprehensive urban plan for a three-hundred-block area of the Bronx. The project included civic, corporate, community, and political leaders who met regularly to develop plans and recommendations. Participants in the project were guided by the principles that planning must begin from the bottom up, planning must be interdisciplinary and comprehensive, economic and social revitalization of the Bronx Center must bring benefits to the immediate community and city, and one measure of future success would be how it provided learning opportunities for the community. The president of HCC chaired the work group on education, culture, and recreation, which was dedicated to incorporating lifelong learning throughout the Bronx Center. Recommendations developed by this group included the following: (1) develop high schools with specialized educational themes; (2) use schools as community centers for adult education, recreation, and other activities; (3) allow public access to the Police Academy and Court Complex educational and athletic facilities; and (4) establish an education consortium to encourage cooperative efforts of diverse Bronx Center groups.

DANA SCOTT PETERMAN is a doctoral student at the University of California Los Angeles Graduate School of Education and Information Studies, and the User Services Coordinator for the ERIC Clearinghouse for Community Colleges.

CAROL A. KOZERACKI is assistant director of the ERIC Clearinghouse for Community Colleges.

INDEX

Access: American educational ideals and, 10; economic health and, 10; excellence and, 32; to learning, 81–82; technology and, 10; urban community college goal of, 6. *See also* Open admissions

Accountability: Community College of Baltimore County and, 82; defining educational, 11; Los Angeles Community College District and, 65; remedial education and, 11; of urban community colleges, 8, 11–12

Adams, J., 87

Affirmative action programs, 44

African Americans: at Borough of Manhattan Community College, 26; at City University of New York, 25–27; at Community College of Denver, 6; in community colleges, 71; at Los Angeles community colleges, 7, 58; in Miami, 15–16; at Seattle community colleges, 43–44, 50; welfare and, 12

AFT Faculty Guild, 65

Ambron, J., 35

American cities. *See* Cities

Anderson, J. R., 35

Arenson, K. W., 28, 32, 33

Asians: at Community College of Denver, 6; at Los Angeles community colleges, 57; at Seattle community colleges, 43–44

Atomistic paradigm, of instruction, 81

August, B., 35

Babbitt, M., 36

Baltimore County: job loss in, 77; population changes in, 76–77; post–World War II growth of, 76; poverty in, 76–77; suburban growth in, 76; urban decline in, 76

Barr, R. B., 76

Basinger, J., 32

Bautsch, J., 43

Biggins, C. M., 91

Blacks. *See* African Americans

Borough of Manhattan Community College (BMCC), 9, 25–26

Brawer, F. B., 7

Brint, S., 29

Bronx Community College (BCC), 25

Building College and Community Services for Single Parents and Displaced Homemakers Project, 86

Business partnerships: at Miami-Dade Community College, 17–19; learning college and, 82; at Maricopa community colleges, 68; at Miami-Dade Community College, 18; at Seattle community colleges, 8–9, 49, 51

California Citizens Commission on Higher Education, 61

California Community Colleges, 56

California State Auditor, 60, 62

"Call for Excellence in Urban Education" (Sainz and Biggins), 91

Campus Compact, 69

Carter, H. M., 7

Chaffee, J., 36

Change, vision and, 79

Charter schools, 71–72

Cheng, M. M., 7

Child care, in community colleges, 9

Cities: demographics of, 6; growth of, 7; immigrants and, 6–7; megacities and, 7; migration and, 7; population changes in, 7; poverty in, 15; sense of community in, 12; suburban growth and, 7. *See also* by specific city

Citizenship preparation: at Los Angeles community colleges, 65; in urban community colleges, 12

City University of New York (CUNY): Kingsborough Community College, 26; access issues at, 24, 26, 32–33; African American students at, 25–27; Borough of Manhattan Community College, 25–26; Bronx Community College, 25; career programs at, 29; College Discovery program and, 26; College Now program and, 36; College of Staten Island, 25; College Prepartory Initiative and, 36; *Community College Review* and, 29; community colleges of, 23, 25; community partnerships at, 31–32; contemporary issues of, 32–37; continuing

95

Back Issue/Subscription Order Form

Copy or detach and send to:
Jossey-Bass Inc., Publishers, 350 Sansome Street, San Francisco CA 94104-1342

Call or fax toll free!
Phone 888-378-2537 6AM-5PM PST; Fax 800-605-2665

Back issues: Please send me the following issues at $25 each
(Important: please include series initials and issue number, such as CC90)

1. CC _____

_____

_____

$ _____ Total for single issues

$ _____ Shipping charges (for single issues *only;* subscriptions are exempt
from shipping charges): Up to $30, add $5^{50} • $30^{01}–$50, add $6^{50}
$50^{01}–$75, add $7^{50} • $75^{01}–$100, add $9 • $100^{01}–$150, add $10
Over $150, call for shipping charge

Subscriptions   Please ❑ start   ❑ renew my subscription to *New Directions
for Community Colleges* for the year 19___ at the following rate:

❑ Individual $60   ❑ Institutional $107
NOTE: Subscriptions are quarterly, and are for the calendar year only.
Subscriptions begin with the spring issue of the year indicated above.
For shipping outside the U.S., please add $25.

$ _____ Total single issues and subscriptions (CA, IN, NJ, NY and DC
residents, add sales tax for single issues. NY and DC residents must
include shipping charges when calculating sales tax. NY and Canadian
residents only, add sales tax for subscriptions)

❑ Payment enclosed (U.S. check or money order only)
❑ VISA, MC, AmEx, Discover Card #_____ Exp. date_____

Signature _____ Day phone _____
❑ Bill me (U.S. institutional orders only. Purchase order required)
Purchase order #_____

Name _____
Address _____

_____

_____

Phone_____ E-mail _____

For more information about Jossey-Bass Publishers, visit our Web site at:
www.josseybass.com   **PRIORITY CODE = ND1**